Packing Your Parachute

Packing Your Parachute

Changing the Way Executives Buy Business Insurance

- Competence before Crisis
- A Terrible Master but an Excellent Servant
- It Was Not Raining When Noah Built the Ark
- Meet Your Silent Partner
- Chalk, Cheese, and the Serial Shopper
- Coverage Mulligans and the Cavalry
- It's All Fun and Games
- The Bystander Effect
- Busy Ants Don't Miss Many Picnics
- All Hat, No Cattle
- The Insurance Audition
- Venial and Mortal Sins
- Autocorrect Can Go Straight to He'll
- Sticks and Stones and Insured Names
- Budgets and the Light at the End of the Tunnel
- Dancing the Foxtrot
- A World without Insurance
- The Policyholder's Bill of Rights
- A Stick and a Begging Purse
- A Different Kettle of Fish

Michael Hale

Copyright © 2017 by Michael Hale.

Library of Congress Control Number:		2017912486
ISBN:	Hardcover	978-1-5434-4389-9
	Softcover	978-1-5434-4390-5
	eBook	978-1-5434-4391-2

All rights reserved. No part of this book may be reproduced or transmitted in any form or by any means, electronic or mechanical, including photocopying, recording, or by any information storage and retrieval system, without permission in writing from the copyright owner.

Any people depicted in stock imagery provided by Thinkstock are models, and such images are being used for illustrative purposes only.
Certain stock imagery © Thinkstock.

Print information available on the last page.

Rev. date: 08/17/2017

To order additional copies of this book, contact:
Xlibris
1-888-795-4274
www.Xlibris.com
Orders@Xlibris.com
765271

Contents

Preface: Competence before Crisis xi

Chapter 1: Money Is a Terrible Master but an Excellent Servant ... 1
Chapter 2: It Wasn't Raining When Noah Built the Ark 3
Chapter 3: Meet Your Silent Partner 5
Chapter 4: Chalk, Cheese, and the Serial Shopper 11
Chapter 5: Coverage Mulligans and the Cavalry 17
Chapter 6: It's All Fun and Games until Santa Checks
the Naughty List 23
Chapter 7: The Bystander Effect 31
Chapter 8: Busy Ants Don't Miss Many Picnics 35
Chapter 9: All Hat, No Cattle 39
Chapter 10: The Insurance Audition 45
Chapter 11: Venial and Mortal Sins in Insurance 51
Chapter 12: Autocorrect Can Go Straight to He'll 61
Chapter 13: Sticks and Stones Can Break Bones, but
Names *Will* Also Hurt 65
Chapter 14: Due to Budget Cuts, the Light at the End
of the Tunnel Is Now Off 71
Chapter 15: Dancing the Foxtrot while Your
Professionals Are Doing the Rumba 75
Chapter 16: A World without Insurance 77
Chapter 17: A Stick and a Begging Purse 81
Chapter 18: The Policyholder's Bill of Rights 83
Chapter 19: A Different Kettle of Fish 87

Notes 91
Index 93

I will keep constantly in mind that until men grow wings, their parachutes must be dependable.

—The Rigger's Pledge
US Army Quartermaster Foundation

Michael S. Hale, Esq., JD, CPCU, AAI

PREFACE

Competence before Crisis

This book's mission is to capture the attention of executives on why the way they may be buying business insurance could be all wrong—perhaps calamitously wrong.

Not many people complain of parachutes failing. It is usually too late. Like parachutes, inadequate insurance programs are often discovered posthaste following a catastrophe, much to the surprise of many executives. Yet many such insurance buyers simply do not have adequate information or advice from which to effectively design or implement such a program.

In Daniel H. Pink's *New York Times* best seller *To Sell is Human*,[1] in analyzing sales processes he refers to the concept of "asymmetrical available information," which he uses to explain that compared to the seller, the buyer is usually at an information disadvantage. Citing the example of the used-car salesman, Pink points out that many times, only the seller knows whether the vehicle is a lemon or a peach, with the buyer being at least partially in the dark, albeit marginally less so in the Information Age.

This publication expands on this theory, making the case that the insurance-buying process inherently involves asymmetrical information, with the buyer often on the short end of the stick. This can lead to major problems for the executive buying the insurance who may not know the precise details of what is being purchased yet is bound to the terms and conditions of the policies.

There is asymmetrical information between the insurance buyer and the seller, and without a competent insurance adviser or agent, an educated decision is very difficult to make when comparing proposals and policies. Even if the buyer understands something about insurance, he or she may not know the endorsements or options that are then available in the industry.

Not only have we sold insurance to some of the largest companies in the world, we have also purchased insurance for many companies throughout the country as consultants and attorneys. We have seen far too many cases where incompetence and inattention to detail have resulted in substantial uninsured or underinsured losses, some of which have claimed the life of the business and a few of which bankrupted the business owner personally.

We have found that *competence cannot be created at the time of a crisis* when it comes to insurance. It must exist not only before a loss but also in an almost paranoidly consistent manner, throughout the negotiation and management of the commercial insurance program.

Put another way, it's usually too late at the time of a major claim to correct the coverage problems that resulted from inattention and lack of proper advice. The policy contracts cannot be reformed to include better language at that time. The limits can no longer be increased for an additional charge. The conditions cannot be renegotiated. The policy language is frozen in time and is not going to be dethawed by the magic wand of wishful thinking in most cases. Perhaps most importantly, the insurance agent and consultant cannot be retroactively reselected.

The elite and renowned Navy SEAL warriors spend countless hours training for the unexpected so that they collectively have the competence necessary at the time of a military crisis. They are prepared, educated, trained, conditioned, and full of anticipation for the worst possible situations. Their parachutes are expertly packed by the best of the best. They are disaster ready by assuming that a crisis will happen. The insurance industry and its customers alike can learn from this kind of thinking.

As we have come to know after being involved in thousands of claims over many years, the problem involves a fundamental failure to undertake forward-thinking risk management measures, which include carefully negotiated insurance policies by qualified experts. This process cannot be accomplished alone. It requires an informed buyer, an accomplished and seasoned broker, an insurance consultant, and the advice and counsel of the firm's CPAs and attorneys.

According to *Inc.* magazine, companies should consider between 20 and 30 percent of predicted gross sales as the baseline budget for comprehensive coverage, including employee benefits.[2] However, this depends on the type of business, with some posing more risk and thus generating higher premiums than others and vice versa.

These costs are staggering, which make it unsurprising that executives treat the purchase of insurance with disdain. This often leads to management looking carefully at these line items and contributes to the desire to shop the insurance. As we examine in this book, negotiating and designing property and casualty insurance to eliminate common problems may not make any significant difference in corporate insurance costs. Doing it right does not always cost more. For example, including all appropriate entities on policies may not cost anything, yet we find that missing names are a problem that plagues many business insurance policies.

We write this book as an antivirus scanning program of sorts for executives to use in analyzing whether a business insurance agency is properly packing the company's parachute. Having a third party audit the current policies as part of an insurance audition is one of the best ways to determine whether the business would suffer a virus that could send executives running for competence at the time of a crisis.

There are, of course, many fine insurance agencies and extremely qualified insurance agents who are more than competent both before and at the time of a client's claim crisis. However, we also find that most buyers do not know if this is the case because they don't know exactly how to buy commercial insurance. Understandably, it is not what they do.

We previously authored two books—*Insurance & Risk* and its previous incarnation, *Always & Nevers*. In these books, we took it on ourselves to attempt to explain what specific types of coverage a business should have. Those publications were well received by many companies and business insurance agents alike. Yet the book you are reading is more about the process than the procedures because we have learned that the technical coverage matters are more within the gambit of the insurance professional, whereas the larger problem of how to buy insurance and who to buy it from are worthier questions for the executive.

In 2016, there were 285,480 insurance sales professionals in the United States.[3] They all want to sell you insurance. We find that far fewer, however, help companies *buy* it. Think about the number of insurers that advertise on cable networks daily. Think about how many cold calls you receive from insurance agents asking to quote your business.

Would you rather have a competent agent quote your insurance with multiple insurance companies and make recommendations to you or ask multiple order-taker agencies to quote your insurance? Which one(s) would or could properly pack your businesses' parachute? It is our experiences that suggest that this may be one of the most critical decisions that can be undertaken by businesses.

Insurance is complicated. So are the risks that generate the more than $25,000,000,000 market for it in the property and casualty insurance industry. We find few buyers with the requisite background or knowledge to be able to effectively negotiate and purchase commercial insurance, and in fact, many do not entirely know what they are getting when they order the policies. It is a sad commentary that this can also be said of even some insurance "producer" agents who are selling the policies.

Insurance policies are not fungible commodities. In many cases, they are as different as chalk and cheese. Many buyers of insurance attempt to obtain quotes "apples-to-apples" when buying insurance policies. With some minor exceptions, there is no such thing.

Thoughtful consideration should be given by those with the unenviable tasks of buying business insurance to be as knowledgeable as possible at the time of coverage negotiation and to secure the most competent of advisers to assist in the process.

More often than not, we find that the insurance-buying process can be a rudderless endeavor, lacking a clear direction on the evaluation of policies in relation to exposures. It is astonishing to us that some insurance agents on whom the buyer relies also lack the proficiency to be able to properly protect the assets of the client organization.

The insurance industry utilizes a peculiar business model where contracts designed to transfer legal risks (a.k.a. policies) are sold, in most cases, by nonlawyers. In point of fact, it only takes about as many hours to get a driver's license motorcycle endorsement as it does to obtain a property and casualty insurance license to sell such risk-transfer contracts that protect businesses, not to mention families. This is not like selling vacuum cleaners with a disclaimer in the box. In the case of the insurance industry, the contract *is* the product.

Business insurance is often purchased, in part, to satisfy other contractual requirements of the insured company, which sometimes include complicated indemnity provisions in lengthy documents. Many times, insurance policies do not track with such contracts that are usually entered into before the insurance is reviewed with little, if any, input from the agent.

Sometimes part of the risk comes from the actual insurance policies themselves. Do you read yours? Your insurers do, as do their stable of attorneys. Many policyholders may not know that a sizable number of insurance policies are written in template form by the insurance industry itself through the Insurance Services Office (ISO). These standardized-form policies take advantage of the economies of scale of this colossal industry that designs policies with an eye toward making them unambiguous—often to the benefit of the insurer. Yet in our experience, they are equally obtuse. The statute of at least one state allows as small as 8-point type in insurance policies.[4]

Many buyers of insurance think that whatever the agent tells them about the policy will be binding upon the insurer if there is misinformation that leads to a gap in coverage. In actuality, it may be the opposite of this. Whatever your insurance agent tells the insurance company is usually binding upon the insured given that the independent insurance agent is the agent of the insured in many states, except where that agent is an employee of the insurance company.

It is also surprising to us how many insurance agents we have encountered that rely on statements from their insurance company underwriters in determining the existence of coverage. Of course, insureds must read their policies, and even if they do not, they are bound to the contract terms anyway. Furthermore, according to the plain terms of virtually all policies, a representative's statements do not amend the policy language. Only a signature by an authorized agent of the insurer can do that.

In some ways, the insurance agent can be more important than the insurance company, which will typically only write a policy the way the agent requests it to be written with or without key endorsements, names, etc. It is uncommon for an insurer to voluntarily extend special coverage and broaden endorsements where it is not requested to do so on an application that is typically filled out by the agent.

The technological developments of our society have led to the availability of so-called five-minute insurance policies, which can be purchased over the Internet. This has only exposed the buyer to further problems as there is no agent to look to for advice or direction or to sue if the coverages were inadequate.

In this book, we discuss real-life stories of disasters that, in some cases, have destroyed businesses and their owners. These stories are largely based on experiences attorneys and insurance expert witness in cases where an improperly designed insurance program led to years of litigation and unimaginable costs.

Executives might be surprised to know that their company's directors' and officers' liability insurance policy may not cover their errors or omissions in decisions about insurance programs. This is all the more reason to spend quality time with competent advisers on understanding options and reviewing coverages, at least annually.

Risk management includes—yet is not exclusive of—buying insurance. However, too many companies we encounter consider the purchase of insurance as the way they manage their risks. Some insurance agents myopically look at it through the same lens. Yet time spent on avoiding, reducing, limiting, or transferring organizational risks, in addition to buying insurance, can pay huge dividends in perpetuating the business as a going concern.

Moreover, such tools can reduce the actual costs of the insurance itself. Put simply, insurance companies are really the insured's silent partners. They like to see noninsurance measures used in protecting against risk. In this way, we provide some noninsurance risk management thoughts toward the end of this book.

In the end, our research and study of the insurance industry over many years tells us that business coverages are often given the short end of the executive's stick when compared with other matters like generating sales, making payroll, and paying taxes. These executives may not be fully to blame. The glut of sales agent order-takers claiming to save them 25 percent in premiums with equivalent coverages likely contributes to why the same executives buy insurance the way they buy janitorial supplies.

The haze of the kaleidoscope through which the executive looks at buying insurance often comes better into focus at the time of an insurer's denial of a claim when not only are the policies dusted off and finally read but agents, attorneys, and others are assembled to attempt to save the day. The process should be the opposite, with competence existing *before* the crisis.

Undoubtedly, some will say that this book is an unjustifiably forlorn look at insurance buying, that insurers are generally not out to get their policyholders, that agents are professionals that cannot be the guarantors of risk for anything that happens to a company it sells insurance to, that policyholders should read their policies and ask questions. To these assertions, what do we say? We wholeheartedly agree!

We do not take on the insurance industry and its players as some dilatory, arcane trade of incompetents. We instead desire only to raise the bar for such professionals and insureds alike so that they look at the processes of buying insurance and managing risk in a different way.

We think that it is time for a different kettle of fish with how business insurance is purchased.

1

Money Is a Terrible Master but an Excellent Servant

P. T. Barney of the famed Barnum & Bailey Circus coined the phrase that "money is a terrible master but an excellent servant."

The insurance industry is certainly an excellent servant to the world's economies in driving progress, supporting financial markets, facilitating credit, and of course, in disaster recovery. To put it simply, it has a *massive* impact.

Check out these statistics.[5] The insurance industry

- employs about 2.5 million people in the US,
- had property and casualty investments of $1.5 trillion in 2015,
- had US payrolls of $247 billion in 2015,
- contributed 2.6 percent of US GDP in 2014, and
- at the end of 2015, had $680.6 billion in surplus.

The availability of insurance plays a key role in providing a backstop for companies to recover from potentially ruinous disasters and enables bank loans, leasing of real and personal property, building construction, and many other areas.

According to the National Association of Insurance Commissioners, there were 5,930 domestic insurance companies in the US in 2015—2,544 of which were property and casualty insurers.[6]

The options available for policies, coverage forms, endorsements, notices, loss control requirements, and claims handling procedures is baffling, to put it mildly. It is unlikely that even the most sophisticated executives could effectively compare all the offerings, especially without having the policies that are being proposed.

As you read this book, consider that, as a funding mechanism and for other reasons such as loss control, the insurance industry is a great servant to businesses such as yours. However, the options for insurers, products, and services in this industry are simply as expansive as they are complex. Yet these products are necessary to almost every company as tools to be used in packing their parachutes. They need to be evaluated, negotiated, and designed accordingly.

2

It Wasn't Raining When Noah Built the Ark

A bolt out of the blue. "It won't happen to me." This natural human trait is referred to as the optimism bias.[7] We generally expect that bad things, such as fires, will come to visit others before us.

In the familiar biblical story of Noah's ark, Noah built his ship over a period of years *before* the great flood. He was planning because he had forewarning from a pretty reliable source of what was to come. We usually do not benefit from such advance notice of things certain to come.

Compare the RMS *Titanic*'s maiden voyage on April 10, 1912, when 2,224 passengers boarded the ship believed to be unsinkable, which five days later would be on the floor of the Atlantic. No one expected this possibility, not even the ship's designer or captain. It would not and could not happen to this ship. It would not and could not happen to this crew. It would not and could not happen to these passengers.

The exact amount of the *Titanic* property loss is hard to ascertain today. Although there were construction costs of $7,500,000, the hull was only insured by Lloyds of London for $5,000,000 with a deductible of 15 percent of the value. The premium was 7 million pounds. All told, Lloyds paid $16,000,000 for such claims in 1912.[8]

Shortly after the tragedy, the ship's designer was quoted as saying that everything that could reasonably be thought of was done to minimize the risk of an *ordinary* accident. Even the captain is believed before the trip to have denied the possibility of this risk occurring due to the strength of the ship, saying,

> But in all my experience, I have never been in any accident of any sort worth speaking about. I have seen but one vessel in distress in all my years at sea. I never saw a wreck and never have been wrecked nor was I ever in any predicament that threatened to end in disaster of any sort.[9]

The captain had optimism bias.

Many business leaders look at their risks in an analogous way, believing that any claim worth speaking about will not happen and that if it does, the chances are that it will not be significant.

This does not mean that the company should be paralyzed by paranoia, of course, lest they will soon be out of business. But our experiences tell us that, at least as to commercial insurance, sometimes the needed fixes are not realized until disaster strikes.

If it does happen to us, the first reaction is often to be thankful that we bought a great insurance policy that will take care of the problem. We hope.

It is well worth the effort to concentrate on building our corporate arks before it starts to rain. We need to *expect* that loss *will* happen, and act accordingly. That process is now.

3

Meet Your Silent Partner

Companies should look at insurers as their silent partners. The insurers certainly do. That's why they demand copious information before agreeing to insure you. That's why they require signed applications they could potentially use against you later if the information is inaccurate. That's why they do loss-control surveys at your facility, and on and on. It's all part of their due diligence of being a stakeholder in your business. They literally judge you on whether they want to be in business with you.

Less commonly do we see the insured companies doing similar due diligence on their own agent or insurer before agreeing to be their partners. Would you want to be a silent partner with your insurer?

Once the deal is done and the policies are issued, you might not have a lot of interaction with that insurer unless there is a claim. The same may be true as to your insurance agent. Sure, there may be inspections, invoices, endorsements, and premium audits, but rarely will the carrier discuss your coverages with you. It holds the figurative pot of gold until something happens. That promise of a pot of gold is the investment from your silent partner, with the terms of that promise appearing in the insurance policy language. Just as you would a silent partner shareholder in your business, you want insurers who will invest in your business both monetarily and with a mind toward maintaining the business as a going concern.

It should be noted that among the thousands of business insurers throughout the country, each has its own policy forms and endorsements. If you counted up the words in the various policies, you would see that some may have three thousand words and some maybe two thousand words. Which is better? How would you know?

In evaluating an insurer, you want to carefully consider whether the policy forms it uses are specialized or standard Insurance Services Office (ISO) forms with modifying endorsements. We recently worked with an insurer that excluded foundations from covered property in the building insurance and did not have an automatic extended endorsement to add such coverage back.

The better insurers are those that have broader forms and extensions, and sometimes even those that do not use ISO forms. The problem is that as a buyer, most executives would not be able to know this without the input of a qualified expert.

Another consideration is the financial strength and size of the insurer. Some insurers are regional insurers, only writing coverages in certain states. Some are national and others international in scope. Which are better?

Your products or business activities can cause a liability that you do not even know of until subsequent years. You need an insurance company that is strong enough to be able to survive in order to pay these claims in future years. An example of this is Kemper Insurance Company. If your liability insurance was with Kemper in 2003 and a liability claim accrued in that year, Kemper would have not been able to pay for that claim because it became insolvent that year.

We know this sounds surprising, but insurance companies do become insolvent or otherwise go out of business. Several of these insurers in the not-so-recent past were over one hundred years old with fine reputations, yet they became insolvent and failed to pay hundreds of millions of dollars of claims, leaving state-managed insolvency funds to step in.

If you look at Kemper in 1998, it had an A.M. Best rating of A or excellent. That A rating was consistent until 2001. In the brief period between 2001 and 2003, Kemper had its rating reduced to D and became insolvent.

There are a number of organizations that provide financial ratings of insurers, including A.M. Best and Fitch. These are largely relied on by companies and are good benchmarking tools. However, your insurance agency should also be closely monitoring the financial stability of the insurer because it has access to substantial information on insurer trends.

When an insurance company is rated A, it is two steps away from a B+. If, for example, there is a major downturn, its rating could go down to A- and then could go to B+. When the rating goes to B+, it typically results in insolvency of the insurance company because all its insureds flee to other insurance carriers when they can, leaving only the higher-risk accounts that are not desirable and cannot leave.

Another tool to consider the financial strength of the insurer is its combined ratio. This is the ratio of earned premiums to losses and expenses incurred, but it does not reflect investment income. For example, in 1998, Kemper paid almost $1.08 in claims payments and operating expenses as compared to every dollar received. If it did not make up the 0.08-cent deficit with investment income, it would be losing money for its shareholders.

Companies that depend on investment income to survive generally want to increase the premiums they write to invest the dollars. In order to write premiums, they have to be very competitive to take the account away from another insurance company. This will exacerbate matters because the underwriting income, which is the difference between the premiums and losses, will go down and will not necessarily be offset by investment income as the insurer underprices accounts in order to write more business. This downward spiral is reflected in the combined ratio.

It is important to note that not all insurers fall within the guarantee funds of the states. Unadmitted or unlicensed insurers generally do not. This does not necessarily mean that an unlicensed insurer is bad. Sometimes an insurer that is very viable financially does not want to be licensed in a particular state because it can offer more variety in its rates and policy forms.

Another thing to think about in evaluating whether an insurer should be your silent partner is whether the insurance carrier has the *willingness* to pay a valid claim promptly and without litigation. In many states, bad faith causes of action are not recognized.

One of the most common statements we hear when it comes to suing an insurer is that the insured wants to recover their attorneys' fees from the insurer for having to sue it. This usually does not happen because the general rule is that the litigants pay their own attorneys' fees, absent a few exceptions. Most cases are settled before any trial on the issue of coverage, so the recovery of legal fees usually does not enter the picture. This is all the more reason to have an insurer that has an attitude of being your silent partner for valid claims.

It is interesting that one fire-claims plaintiff law firm told us that they would not have their own law firm insurance or personal insurance with certain carriers because of their experiences with them. This says a lot.

Would your insurer start the claims adjustment process as a woman scorned—not trusting anyone and hardened to the process? This is not to say that insurers always turn down valid claims. However, it is good to know the claims-paying philosophy and history of the insurer you are considering as your silent partner. A good insurance agent will share both objective information about this, as well as his or her experiences on other claims. Use this information to your advantage.

Meet our client Rachel, an engineer. Rachel had a major water-damage loss at her home. The insurer not only refused to cover the loss, claiming that she was not living there at that particular time, it also said that there was a misrepresentation on her application and sent her a letter rescinding the policy and returned her money. In her words, "I felt like a criminal."

Many public adjusters will tell you that they know which insurers will argue hard at the time of a fire claim to heavily and unreasonably depreciate assets that they insured so as to minimize the payout. This is not the kind of silent partner that you want.

Be cautious about moving your business insurance to an insurer based on price alone. A knee-jerk reaction has risks of its own. Here are a few examples:

a. There is the risk that the new insurance carrier will become insolvent and cancel midterm. Most insurance carriers can cancel without any reason with only ten to thirty days' notice, depending on the type of policy, and may fail to return prepaid premiums or pay claims.
b. There is the risk that after writing an account, the new carrier will have a change in appetite or buyer's remorse and will either cancel your account midterm or not renew at the next renewal date again.
c. The new insurance carrier may terminate doing business with the agent with which you do business.
d. The new insurance carrier will likely perform payroll or sales audits differently, resulting in major additional premiums retroactively applied if it is not similar to how your current insurer operates.
e. The new insurance carrier may cancel your account after one major claim.
f. The new insurance carrier may inspect your locations after the business has been placed and then want to cancel the policies midterm with only thirty days' notice because they do not like what they see or they insist on significant and expensive improvements.
g. The new insurance carrier may find that the agent misrepresented the account and cancels midterm or denies a claim.

    h. The coverages are less than the previous carrier provided, but you do not determine this until you have a claim.

    i. The new insurance carrier checks driving records and excludes drivers that were previously acceptable because of different underwriting standards.

Evaluate insurers—and as subsequently discussed in this book, insurance agents—by considering this question:

> Would this company be the kind of silent partner of our business that we would want?

For one reason: It will be.

4

Chalk, Cheese, and the Serial Shopper

There are many executives who treat insurance like commodities such as wood, wire, janitorial supplies, toilet paper, etc. Those same executives might take a far different approach when making decisions about other aspects of their lives. Think about the following.

Would you do any of the following?

- Go into the emergency room and ask for the cheapest doctor because your deductible and co-pay had not been met.
- Utilize a physician that never asks questions or gathers the necessary information to design a medical program to keep your most important asset (your body) viable.
- Pick the attorney with the lowest hourly rate to solve a major problem and protect the company's assets.
- Use the US Post Office for next-day delivery rather than pay a little more money for an overnight mail delivery service such as Federal Express.
- Hire the least-expensive executives to work for you to make the best decisions regarding their company.
- Ask for bids from your accounting adviser and select the one with the lowest cost.

For most people, the answer is—of course not.

Yet we often find that the insurance-buying process is heavily weighted in favor of the lowest-cost provider. To make it worse, the buyer becomes a serial shopper by bidding the account every year.

The serial insurance shopper will eventually find an insurance program that is cheaper. Let's face it. They always can. There is usually a commission-only agent out there that will find a way to save money for a buyer, at least in the short term.

There is one thing for sure that all insurance policies have in common. They are different—all of them. In many ways, comparing them is like comparing chalk and cheese. That is why the idea that an agent should quote apples-to-apples what the insured has in place is fallacious thinking.

Terms and conditions of coverage always vary as much as the insurers issuing the policies. Insuring agreements are not always the same— different exclusions, different endorsements, different conditions, different number of words.

Attention, buyers. When you buy insurance, you are buying a contract. That's what a policy is. Are all leases the same? All renovation construction contracts? All purchase agreements? Hardly. Yet oddly, we often find that many insurance buyers treat the purchase of it as if they were buying a commodity.

If the process of buying insurance was like purchasing janitorial supplies, the insurer with the best premium should win the account every time. It is really about terms and conditions, which can only be properly understood by a seasoned insurance professional.

Despite the above, many selling agents will tell you that the coverage being quoted is the same as what you have. Such statements should be carefully considered because they are not likely to be binding upon the insurer in many states, unless the agent is an employee of the insurance company. Here's what's interesting. Most executives do not know this.

Check out the case of the barbershop, one of the first cases this author handled as an insurance attorney years ago. In that case, a barber, knowingly or unknowingly, nicked a patron on more than one visit. The patron developed a serious condition called keloids. He sued the barber.

Upon receipt of the lawsuit, the barber breathed a sigh of relief thinking that he had insurance coverage. After all, the insurance agent who sold him the policy told him he had coverage for such incidents. He certainly was surprised when he received a denial letter from the insurer stating that due to a "tonsorial exclusion" he had no coverage on his general liability insurance policy.

Huh? A tonsorial treatment exclusion? He had to look that one up, and he learned that *tonsorial* means "of or relating to beauty treatments." But wait, the agent told him he had coverage, so he retained a lawyer to sue the insurer and that agent.

The barber's case against the insurer was dismissed based not only on the tonsorial exclusion but also because the court determined that even if the agent presented to the barber that he had coverage for this type of claim, he was the legal agent for the insured and not the insurer! Insurer out.

The insurance agent defended the claim by saying he had no duty to advise the barber of anything and he should have read his own policy. Insurance agent out.

Barber and barbershop were on their own, holding the bag for the defense costs and the settlement.

Sad. It could happen to you. Under the laws of virtually all states, you have a duty to read your insurance policy and raise any questions. Even if your independent agent tells you there is coverage, don't rely on that because such statements may not be binding upon the insurer.

What's worse? As a general rule in many states, the insurance agent has no duty to advise you of anything unless they assume such a duty or otherwise have a special relationship with you. It could be different if you are buying insurance from an employee of the insurer, but usually this is not the case for commercial insurance buyers.

If an agent intentionally or innocently misrepresents your account to the insurer or does not disclose all the information that the agent has, that failure could be imputed to you and could contribute to the denial of a claim.

Proposals from independent insurance agencies are often less than comprehensive in scope. In fact, they are usually only a summary of limits, such as building, contents, and general liability. If the buyer does not know what questions to ask to compare the actual coverages, the assumption is often that what they are comparing is the same. In short, they rely on the agent who sold them the policy. This could be a disaster waiting to happen.

Would you enter into a complicated contract with a lot of fine print and technical meaning without checking with a lawyer? Usually not. Most executives do, however, when it comes to buying insurance contracts.

Insurance is one of the only industries we know of where the policy contract being purchased is not received until well after it is purchased. Insurance is usually bought sight unseen. It is critical to actually see the specimen insurance policies that would be issued so you or your insurance adviser can examine the precise language of the four corners of the policies.

The better agencies will look carefully at the policy forms proposed by the insurer and refer to potential coverage issues in the written proposal. If you get a proposal that merely summarizes dollar limits, a red light should go off.

Proposals that highlight gaps, provide explanatory notes and disclaimers, and offer additional coverages send the message that the agent is an adviser and not an order-taker. When it comes to protecting your assets, don't accept any agent who will not commit to this one point from the very start.

We often require agents we oversee for our clients to sign a statement agreeing that they have a special relationship and a duty to advise and are not mere order-takers. Some refuse, saying that their errors and omissions insurance will not allow this. However, this is usually a bad sign, and many times such agents are outed. You should try the same. Ask your agent to sign a statement that he or she and their agency have a special relationship with your business and they agree that they have a duty to advise you on the adequacy of coverage. For a sample, go to www.packingyourparachute.com.

In buying insurance policies, you will typically see insurance proposals that have conditions or subjectivities to what is being proposed. It is advisable to look carefully at this and narrow them down before going with that proposal.

Here are examples of some such subjectivities:

a. *You must submit a business income worksheet before coverage can be bound.* These forms are typically difficult to complete and may require the input from your outside CPA.
b. *Proper insurance to value must be confirmed through a signed statement of values.* Does this mean that the insurance company can come back after they write your insurance and challenge the values and require that you insure higher building values, for example? A signed statement of values can be used against you if the values do not have any rhyme or reason.
c. *Completed and signed applications are required prior to binding.* Applications have many questions. Any one of those questions could be used to deny a loss if they are not complete and fully accurate. When looking at questions and applications, you will see that it is often not possible to give a complete answer, yet it can be used against you if it contains inaccurate information. See our separate chapter "It's All Fun and Games until Santa Checks the Naughty List."

d. *A currently valued five-year loss history is required.* An insurer can later withdraw a quote if it does not like your claims history.
   e. *Subject to inspection.* This means that the insurance company has not seen your operations and might change its mind as to pricing, coverage, or willingness to stay on the account after it does.

As a result, look carefully at subjectivities in proposals before agreeing to move from one insurer to another.

The fine print of an insurance policy can be likened to the contracts that commercial airline flyers are subject to. In the event of any injury or incident that invokes responsibility in the airline, it may refer to the fine print of its contract of carriage. For one major airline, this document is thirty-seven thousand words in a fifty-six-page document. Of course, no one has read such a document except the lawyers who prepared it.

The insurance industry presents a similar quagmire, although at least the insurance policies are somewhat more conspicuous than a hidden contract of carriage that most flyers do not even know about. Nonetheless, even when they read their policies, most executives are not likely to understand the nuances of the fine print of the insurance contract or the hundreds of optional endorsements or other policies that may be available to address coverage gaps.

Therefore, it is important to utilize the services of property and casualty attorneys or advisers in addition to competent insurance agents or brokers. Take the time to understand the insurance policy and to be certain that it is negotiated to cover the risk-of-loss needs of your business.

Many buyers might think that such policies are a lot like the disclaimers in the box of a newly purchased hair dryer—take it or leave it. This may not be the case. Particularly in competitive "soft" markets where insurers have a lot of cash surplus and desire to write new business, it becomes easier to negotiate terms—terms that, when compared, are more like chalk and cheese than apples to apples.

5

Coverage Mulligans and the Cavalry

If you play golf, you know all about mulligans. Forget the prior shot that you sliced into the woods or, worse, that bobbled and barely hit three feet. Don't count that stroke. You can still get to par.

With rare exceptions, you don't get mulligans in insurance despite what may be the reasonable expectations of an insured buyer. Get used to it, and plan accordingly.

Good luck with the expectation that your underwriter will add a correcting endorsement after the fact. Best wishes in asking the claims adjuster to overlook the coinsurance penalty provision in the property policy. They both have someone to answer to at the insurance company that employs them.

You almost certainly won't be getting a do over to add an entity name that your agent left off or to correct a mistake in an application you or your representative signed.

There is no "back to the future" in the insurance game.

The time of a claim is when most people start looking at their policies. Again, a policy is a contract that is not amendable except in writing by an officer of the company.

It's like asking a landlord to retroactively lower the rental rate because business has unexpectedly changed for you. Or like expecting a contractor to add a wall not included in the original drawings because you forgot you needed it. After all, you are a good tenant. You are a good property developer and have worked with the general contractor a lot in the past.

If there is one thing we have learned in many years of practice as insurance attorneys, agents, and consultants, it is that courts reviewing insurance policy disputes will usually decide the matter based on the commonly understood plain language of the words used in the policies. They generally will not consider what the policyholder's reasonable expectations were or what the agent told them. And most of the time, although not always, courts will be loath to find an ambiguity in the policy language.

Insurance is not graded on a curve.

The University of California–Berkeley still grades on a curve that massages academic grades around an average of the class. The theory is that such a curve system creates motivation for students to foster competition.

Trying hard, however, does not always result in the reward of a good grade in the curve system because a student might not get the A due to the average. On the other end of the spectrum, some students who would have gotten a C might be pushed to a B based on what others have done.

We often see policyholders expecting that their claims will be paid "on a bell curve" basis with the benefit of the doubt going to them, comparatively speaking, because they are a better-than-average risk:

- "I'm a better-than-average risk to this insurer."
- "Unlike other insureds, I never turn in claims. This is the first claim I have had."
- "I have been with this insurer for twenty-five years, far longer than most accounts of my type."

- "The automobile accident was not my fault, and I should not be penalized based on the negligence of others."
- "I am an above-average client and am more profitable to the insurer than other accounts."
- "If you do not pay my claim, I am moving my business."

The reality is that insurance claims are not paid based on your underwriting performance in relation to others. How good of a risk you are to the insurer is not part of the formula of the claims adjuster. It just does not work that way in real life.

Ethan Gross, Esq., from Globe Midwest Adjusters Inc., notes that many policyholders believe that the insurance claims adjuster is provided by the insurer as a service to them for the insurance premiums that they paid. He compares this to a belief that the auditor from the Internal Revenue Service is assigned as a service to the taxpayer as part of the tax dollars that he or she paid and is there to help. Neither is true. The adjuster is usually not your friend, nor is the IRS auditor.

The claims department is separate and distinct from the underwriting department. It is the claims adjuster's job to fly speck the claim.

It does not matter how long you have bought insurance from that company, and it does not matter that you are threatening to move the business to another carrier. According to one adjuster we talked with, they hear that one almost every day.

Insurers don't care about claims they might have paid for other policyholders. In fact, they expend considerable effort in coverage litigation attempting to shield the discovery of how other claims were handled.

Instead the adjuster is laser-beam focused on what the policy language says. Rather than looking to what coverages were included for other insureds, the question is what coverages were included on *your* policy.

Will the insurance agent's volume of business with that insurer matter? Maybe, but not usually, because insurers get concerned about setting trends.

Stop thinking that you have leverage at the time of a claim because you are a better-than-average risk, have not had claims in the past, and have been with the insurer a long time. In point of fact, the real measure of leverage of the buyer is at the time the policy was negotiated.

The adjuster will not be influenced by the fact that you did not read your insurance policies and did not understand its terms and conditions.

The adjuster will not be influenced by the total loss of your business and the layoff of all your employees unless the adjuster finds that there is business interruption coverage that applies to this event.

The adjuster will usually not change his or her mind if your insurance agent calls, threatening to remove all its business from this particular insurance company.

The adjuster will not usually care that your insurance agent made a mistake in filling out an application for you or in ordering the policy. The independent agent, in most states, is the agent for the insured, not the insurer.

The adjuster's job is to pay only in accordance with the terms and conditions of the insurance policy that you purchased. This is a contract and is no different from any other written agreement that you may enter.

The adjuster is not in a position to change or overlook any terms and conditions of the policy for a claim that is not consistent with the policy language. They typically like their job too much.

Buyers of products and services usually have preordained expectations of how the process will go and what they will be getting for their money.

For example, most consumers expect:

- Visiting the Apple Store will be a pleasant experience.
- FedEx will be on time, every time.
- McDonald's food will be consistent at restaurants worldwide.
- Amazon's website will be easy to use.
- Google searches will provide the answer.
- The cable repair person will always be late.
- Setting up your wireless and cable TV will be a complicated process.
- Casinos will always be full of smoke.
- Politicians will only tell you what you want to hear and always want money.
- Printed newspapers contain stale news when delivered.
- The washing machine repair person will always tell you that they "don't make parts for that model anymore" and that "you will have to buy a new machine."
- Bad service in a restaurant also means bad food.
- When you call your credit card company or bank, you can expect to always get an automated system of many prompts.
- Going to the dentist will always involve some pain.

The same is true in buying insurance. One of the most common situations we encounter with businesses is the insurance buyer's belief that because they have been with an insurer or agent for many years or paid lots of premium dollars, they will be given the benefit of any doubt at claims time. Here are examples of things we hear all the time:

- All insurance policies are the same, and only the price is different.
- If a major claim happens, our huge insurance company will step up to the plate.
- We have been with the same insurer for twenty years and paid them a lot of premium dollars. They will support us in a crisis.
- If a name is missing on the named insured schedule, the insurance company will overlook it.

- If we find out after an auto accident that a vehicle is in the employee's name and not the company name, the carrier won't make a big deal of it.
- If we accidentally misstated some information on the application for insurance the agent filled out, the insurer won't hold it against us.
- When we called our agent to alert him to the claim, he told us it was covered and there would be no problem and that the statement was binding upon the insurer.
- If we are sued for amounts over our umbrella limits, the insurer will protect us by settling the claim within our limits.
- The agent told us that the insurance company underwriter intended to cover this type of situation, and this supersedes the policy language.

Insurance buyers should understand that the claims department is often completely distinct from the underwriting department, with little sharing of information. While underwriters might want to retain the insured's business, the claims adjuster is usually interested in enforcing the exact policy language regardless of the intentions of the underwriter or the reasonable expectations of the insured.

We often tell our clients that in the event of a claim, especially a large one, they should not expect that the insurer is simply going to show up with a check for the policy limits. We advise them that they should not expect the cavalry to come to immediately rescue them on the day after the fire or wind damage. While this may sound cynical, it reflects the reality of what we see every day in our practices.

The best way to avoid a coverage dispute is to have the policy properly negotiated in the first place, so as to minimize the bullets that you would have to dodge otherwise. Or at a minimum, you should know what you have and what you don't have in terms of coverage.

Concentrate on taking your mulligans at the time you negotiated the policies because they almost always won't exist at claim time.

6

It's All Fun and Games until Santa Checks the Naughty List

One of the worst representations of the insurance industry relates to insurance applications. They are not just traps for the unwary. They are often death traps, asking for a representation of information in questions that no one could ever possibly answer accurately.

It all seems great with insurance until the insurer starts looking closely at your underwriting file following a major claim. Misstatements, misrepresentations, failures to disclose information? The insurer may well find that you are on the naughty list, and you are getting nothing from your policy. In fact, they may try to rescind it ab initio, which is a fancy way of saying "here's your money back. We are tearing up the policy."

Our work as attorneys, insurance expert witnesses, and adjusters allows us to confidently say that alleged misrepresentations or failure to disclose information is one of the most frequent coverage defenses asserted by property and casualty insurance companies in this day and age.

In life insurance, the insurer generally only has two years to determine any misrepresentation. Not so with business insurance, where the insurer has the right to make this assertion at any time.

At the time of a claim, insurers may be quick to pull the rug out from under the policyholder if they find that any information presented was inaccurate, even if the applicant did not intend to defraud the insurer and even if the applicant did not complete the application form. And they may not need to do anything more than send you a letter and return the premium.

Most insurance policies contain some sort of provision governing concealment, misrepresentation, or fraud. These provisions allow the insurance company to void the policy if any insured conceals or misrepresents a material fact relating to coverage, the covered property, their interest in the covered property, or a claim presented under that coverage part.

The actual insurance application also contains a warranty statement that the insured must sign. The following is an excerpt from most standard insurance applications:

> INSURANCE APPLICANT'S STATEMENT
>
> I HAVE READ THE ABOVE APPLICATION AND ANY ATTACHMENTS. I DECLARE THAT THE INFORMATION PROVIDED IN THEM IS TRUE, COMPLETE AND CORRECT TO THE BEST OF MY KNOWLEDGE AND BELIEF. THIS INFORMATION IS BEING OFFERED TO THE COMPANY AS AN INDUCEMENT TO ISSUE THE POLICY FOR WHICH I AM APPLYING.

Insurance companies have the ability to deny coverage if they can establish that the insured misrepresented or concealed material information on the initial application for insurance or during a subsequent claim.

Material generally means that if the insurer had this information, it would have either not agreed to insure the person or company or would have charged a higher premium.

In some cases, we have seen insurers deny coverage for information that was not disclosed by the insured, even if it was not asked on the application!

In one case we were involved with, an insurer denied coverage to its insured after a major fire, stating that the application represented that the building was twenty-six years old when it was really more than fifty years old. The insurer's underwriter testified that the insurer would not have issued replacement cost coverage had it known the right age. That representation, therefore, was material. Interestingly, the applicant did not fill out the application with that inaccurate information; its insurance agent did.

In a May 2017 case filed by an insurance company in California, the insurer pointed to language in the application requiring the insured to disclose any material changes even *after* the application is signed:

> THE APPLICANT AGREES TO NOTIFY THE COMPANY OF ANY MATERIAL CHANGE IN THE ANSWERS TO THE QUESTIONS ON THIS APPLICATION WHICH MAY ARISE PRIOR TO THE EFFECTIVE DATE OF ANY POLICY ISSUED PURSUANT TO THIS APPLICATION AND THE APPLICANT UNDERSTANDS THAT ANY OUTSTANDING QUOTATIONS MAY BE MODIFIED OR WITHDRAWN BASED UPON SUCH CHANGES.[10]

Your eighteen-year-old son lives in your basement. Last year he was convicted of DUI. Since he won't be driving your car, do you have to list him on an insurance application?

Do you have to disclose to the insurance company that your property is vacant?

Your daughter just turned sixteen years old. She only drives your car on the weekends. Since your policy automatically covers family members, do you have to tell the insurance company she is a new driver?

When your insurance company asked about your garaging location, you gave them your parent's address. The premiums would be twice as much if you told them the actual garaging location.

Can't you just underestimate your property insurance values on an application or statement of values to save on premium?

Many times, insurance applications are looked upon as an administrative afterthought. The truth is that applications are one of an insurance company's first lines of defense when attempting to deny a claim.

It gets better—or is it worse? Some insurers make the case that even if the answers were accurate on the application, it is incumbent on an applicant for insurance to inform the insurer of prospective conditions.

In a recent case filed in New Jersey,[11] an insurance company sought to rescind a commercial general-liability insurance policy issued to a subcontractor because an application submitted through the insurance agent for the subcontractor contained inaccurate information. The complaint referred to the answers in boxes checked on the application as inaccurate, such as this one:

> Has the insured been involved in any construction of new residential properties i.e. Custom Homes, in the past ten years.
>
> Answer: No.

Even though it had not done prior work for new residential properties, the insurer alleged that the contractor should have disclosed the fact that it was going to be working on a massive residential construction policy.

Who comes up with these questions used by almost all standard insurers in the property and casualty insurance industry? Some of the questions asked on applications are so vague that it would be virtually impossible to answer them accurately. The following specific examples in standardized applications show how ridiculous some of these inquiries are. They are either designed to trip up the insured or to give the insurer a pocket denial if it needs it.

Here are some examples:

Acord Form 125—Commercial Insurance Application

Any exposure to flammables, explosives, chemicals?

Typically, the answer would be no. However, this would not be correct because every business has exposure to flammables by way of paper, explosives by way of natural gas, and chemicals, which could consist of pool chlorine, cleaning supplies, or other supplies used in the business.

Any catastrophe exposure?

Again, the typical answer is no; however, every risk has a catastrophe exposure of some sort.

Any past losses or claims relating to sexual abuse or molestation allegations, discrimination or negligent hiring?

This is an interesting question as it does not relate to anything that is covered under a commercial general liability insurance policy. Nonetheless, note that it doesn't limit itself to one year or three years but "any past losses relating to sexual abuse or molestation allegations, discrimination or negligent hiring." This language is so broad that it is impossible to answer no over the entire history of the company.

Any uncorrected fire code violations?

How would an insured know if there are any uncorrected fire code violations in the building? If they are a tenant, they would have no way of knowing. We would guess that almost all insureds have some sort of uncorrected fire code violations. Furthermore, you could be in violation of whatever a fire code is but not be required to comply unless the building has a major loss.

Under "Loss History" on this same application, there is a statement:

> Enter all claims or losses (regardless of fault and whether or not insured) or occurrences that may give rise to claims for the prior 5 years.

Claims and losses are two different things. Further, this question isn't even limited to premises liability but would apply to losses that have occurred (or could occur in the future) for workers' compensation and every other area of claims. How do you know what losses could give rise to a future claim? It could be a slip and fall in the parking lot that is not reported and is unknown to management. Note that the question does not relate to "known" claims or losses.

The Commercial General Liability Section of the Acord Application

> Any medical facilities provided or medical professionals employed or contracted?

Most manufacturing facilities, as an example, will have first aid rooms, which means that a medical facility is being provided even though there are no medical professionals employed or contracted.

> Any operations sold, acquired, or discontinued in last 5 years?

Notice that this does not ask about businesses that are sold, acquired, or discontinued. It asks about *operations*. The manufacturing plant or other businesses could have many operations that have been discontinued, so a "no" would be inaccurate.

> Any parking facilities owned/rented?

Certainly, every business has parking facilities, so a "no" would be inaccurate.

> Have any crimes occurred or been attempted on your premises within the last three years?

How would you know whether a potential burglar has attempted to commit a crime on your premises? This crime could be an attempted break-in of automobiles or an attempted break-in of a building.

Acord Form 131—Umbrella

This application asks you to list underlying insurance coverage information, including all restrictions or extensions of coverage. The only way to properly comply with this is to attach a copy of all underlying policies.

Acord Form 127—Business Auto Section

> Any hold harmless agreements?

There are almost certainly hold harmless agreements in every business, many of which require that an insured hold someone else harmless for automobile-type claims.

> Any vehicles used by family members? If so, identify in remarks.

Any commercial vehicle could be used by a family member of someone.

> Are any drivers not covered by workers' compensation?

How would you know?

> Any drivers with convictions for moving traffic violations?

Seldom do we see an account where drivers would not have convictions for moving traffic violations.

Acord 130—Workers' Compensation

> Any employees under 16 or over 60 years of age?

Seldom will a business not have employees who are over the age of sixty.

> Any employees with physical handicaps?

Aside from the discriminatory aspects of this question, everyone has some sort of physical handicap.

If you lost a fingertip, does this constitute a handicap? If you have an impaired field of vision yet your eyesight is twenty-twenty, is this a physical handicap?

Failure to read the policy is not a defense to a material misrepresentation in an insurance application.

Statements made by your insurance agent in preparing an insurance application are usually going to be binding upon the policyholder even if the policyholder never even saw the application.

The best advice is to not complete the Acord applications except the top portion of the Acord 125, the "Applicant Information" section. Indicate "see attached" and attach schedules and account information and don't answer any of these impossible-to-answer questions.

It's easy to get on the naughty list if you are not careful with insurance applications.

7

The Bystander Effect

There's a phrase sometimes used by psychologists called the bystander effect. When a group of people observe an emergency, like a fire or a mugging, there's a tendency for them to believe that someone else has the situation under control. Someone else is probably calling the fire department. Somebody else will probably find a police officer. Someone else is going to get the automatic defibulator.

The bystander effect is apparent in the business world too. Let's say you have two lists of tasks: one list is directly assigned to you, while the other is up for grabs for anyone on your team. Psychologically, you're more likely to cross things off your own list before you worry about the team list.

Organizations, their management, and their outside professionals, such as law firms, accounting firms, and consultants, are often plagued with the bystander effect in thinking that someone else has the management of risk under control. Examples of this include the following:

- "Our attorney has addressed our exposure to employee lawsuits, and we are protected."
- "Our purchasing department has contingencies in place to get raw materials if there is a fire at our usual supplier's facility."

- "The company's general counsel has provided all entity names to the insurance agent."
- "The limited liability company's CPA has reviewed our business interruption exposures, and our limits of insurance and coverages are adequate."
- "Our financial advisers have our financial statements and would have us increase our umbrella limit if that were needed."

Our favorite is this:

- "Our insurance agent is a professional and has us properly insured."

These statements, which we hear frequently in our work with agents, companies, and as expert witnesses, are alarming. Here are two examples of real-life examples of this bystander effect involving lawyers representing a business:

Scenario one. A twenty-thousand-square-foot multimillion-dollar commercial office building is the subject of an electrical fire and is a total loss. The leases that the company's lawyer drafted contained insurance requirements provisions but also included a section allowing the tenants to terminate the lease if more than 50 percent of the building was damaged. It is an especially bearish real-estate market, and the building owner is concerned about rerenting the building once it is rebuilt, which he anticipates will take eighteen months considering the ordinance issues. The major tenants are canceling their leases per the termination provision. The building owner is advised by his agent that he only has twelve months of coverage for loss of rents. He then calls his attorney to ask why the leases were drafted with such exit clauses. After all, he wrote the lease agreements.

Scenario two. A lawyer advises her manufacturer client that it can limit liability by forming separate limited liability companies for the real estate it owns and for its two separate business divisions. The client agrees, and these entities are formed. Later that year, a lawsuit is filed where all three entities are named defendants. The company comes to learn that the insurance agent had only listed the main entity on the general liability and umbrella policies and did not include the other two names. The lawyer thought the client would advise the insurance agent of the new names, but this did not happen. After the business owner gets the denial letter from the insurer, she asks her attorney why there is now more exposure to her with this entity structure.

These are examples of the bystander effect in insurance and risk management. In both scenarios, the business owner had assumed that the other professionals had addressed the exposures. One hand did not know what the other hand was doing, resulting in an underinsured loss in the first case and an uninsured loss in the second.

In our work as insurance attorneys, agents, and expert witnesses, it is surprising to us how infrequently law firms raise insurance coverage gaps, much less ask to review their client's business insurance policies. They tend to shy away from such matters for fear of liability. We do not see this to be the case as much with accounting firms that do know to ask some insurance-related questions and often talk with their client about matters such as business interruption coverage issues.

Business majors and MBA candidates are not routinely taken aside by professors and told the tricks of the trade in buying business insurance. The same is true for law schools that teach contracts yet pay little heed to the interplay between insurance policies and legal and business exposures.

8

Busy Ants Don't Miss Many Picnics

D on't tell me what to do, how much risk I have, or what I need to buy. I'm busy!

Unsubscribe me. Please.

Stop calling me. Please.

I just want to make payroll this month!

Insurance salespeople are the poster children for interruption marketing—phone calls to obtain expiration dates, meetings set up to purportedly save you 25 percent, requests for voluminous information for underwriting purposes, hundreds of e-mails and advertisements.

We find that many companies cringe at the average insurance agent and their lip service with such statements as these:

- "You need to buy life insurance to protect your family."
- "You should buy environmental insurance."
- "You need to increase your umbrella limits."
- "You must have your contractor give us evidence of insurance."
- "You have no cyber coverage and need it."

Shall we go on?

The average executive is inundated with major tasks and challenges that occupy his or her time; insurance buying is not often at the top of the list, or so it would seem.

Insurance is boring to most buyers. We feel their pain. Currently trending cyber insurance is not exactly fun to talk about. Most commercial insurance buyers are worried about generating revenues, making payroll, and retaining customers.

Consider the ant. You rarely encounter a lazy one. Ants always appear to be decidedly busy building their colonies but don't seem to miss many picnics. Why is that? Perhaps it is because they are more interested in the basics, like survival.

Ant colonies seem to have something in common with business organizations. They show evidence of a division of labor (different ants do different jobs), communication with others, and an almost human ability to solve complex problems. They are also busy all the time, mostly with the tasks of promoting the survival of themselves and the colony.

Over the years, we have found that buying insurance is a lot like this. Executives are busier than ever. They eschew more work being added to their plate in getting loss runs, filling out applications, completing surveys on the business, providing resumes of management, or even reading their policies. They are often more worried about feeding themselves and their employees.

Insurance agents usually create work for their would-be buyers rather than detract from it. It has always amazed this author that blank applications are given to insureds at every renewal when a lot of this information is already in the insurance agent's possession.

We were once told by an executive that in the renewal process, he had counted the number of e-mails received from competing brokers in an effort to determine which one caused him the most work.

Comparatively, attorneys and CPAs usually do a lot of the work for the client instead of creating it for them. They are business advisers more than assigners of busy work to their clients. While some of this is unavoidable with commercial insurance, agents need to try to emulate this model more by focusing on becoming advisers rather than order-taking bidders.

Executives unknowingly contribute to the problem when they agree to quote their insurance every year, retain order-taker insurance agents rather than advisers, and use agencies that make more work for them.

The insurance-buying process needs to be made more interesting, more consultative, and less sales-like. Agents might do so by thinking about the prospect like an ant going to a picnic—interested in its survival, its shelter, and the colony.

9

All Hat, No Cattle

Originally used to reference people who imitate the fashion or style of cowboys, the saying "all hat, no cattle" is often used in the West to refer to those who wear the cowboy hat but have no genuine experience on the ranch.

Many insurance agents, though certainly not all, have similar propensities. Trained as salespeople "producers" first and usually with only a limited number of hours of training, they often lack the necessary background to be able to advise clients on the protection of assets.

The statutes of many states refer to insurance salespeople as *producers*. This is telling. Such licensees are trained from the start to *produce* business as salespersons, meaning that they need to sell as much as possible. This engenders images of manufacturers' representatives selling auto parts. Of course, insurance is far different.

Polished and with glossy brochures in tote, such licensed agents tout the benefits of their company's "great service" and, in one case, responded to our inquiries about coverage for an auto dealer by saying that the insurance company they were selling for "had the broadest policy language available in the industry," all while not being able to explain basic coverage problems like coinsurance penalty provisions, fire sprinkler warranties, and employee-owned vehicles. This is an example of being all hat, no cattle, and it is something that you, as the buyer, want to avoid at all costs.

In our practice that is dedicated to the nuances of business insurance policies and coverages, we see less-than-stellar performances by many insurance agents. Sloppiness seems to be the rule rather than the exception in many instances. Agents are sued for errors or omissions more often than many would think.

We find that while many agents cavalierly define *great service* by how quickly they return calls or e-mails, the more proficient agents judge themselves on how well they advise their clients on the coverages and strive to be more than mere order-takers. The latter are too many in number. Insurance agents, who are often at the center of protecting a company's assets, are only required to take a forty-hour self-study course in many states followed by an examination to be able to legally sell you business insurance.

Marsh, Aon, Willis, Brown & Brown—these are some of the big guys, the largest brokers in the world. Then there is the Robert Smith Agency Inc. Which agency is better? Maybe the better question is, what agent is better?

It is important to have the resources of a sophisticated agency. However, those agencies sometimes adopt the "sell and see ya" approach, with those having the most knowledge doing the selling of the policies and the person with less knowledge in the office taking it from there with occasional input from the producer. This approach maximizes profitability to the agency but tends to minimize quality.

You may have noticed that insurance agencies tend to make a big deal about their teams. On a recent $100,000 account we consulted on, there were two competing proposals.

One agency touted the fact that they would have the following people handle this account:

- Account executive
- Senior vice president
- Account manager
- Assistant account manager

- Claims manager
- Carrier marketing manager

The other agency used these titles:

- Account agent
- Account executive
- Claims specialist

These titles may work to allocate work within the agency, meaning that the agency is structuring its organization to serve *its needs*. However, it may not best serve the client.

One company we visited with said that there were seven vice presidents who came to the sales meeting from the agency. Really?

Our experience is that clients want to, at most, know one or two people at an insurance firm—similar to law firms, CPAs, doctors, banks, and so forth.

Most insurance agencies pay people on a commission basis to bring in and service accounts. It is a produce-or-die arrangement that creates numerous problems such as these:

- Because of the long process it takes to work an account and get paid for it, the account executive getting paid on a commission basis could wait months to get paid, making it difficult to support a family. This also makes it difficult to hire seasoned account executives.
- When a draw is paid, it is typically low, creating a burden on the account executive and creating an incentive for the account executive to write as much business as possible, regardless of the long-term consequences to the agency or the new clients.
- For account executives who are paid on a commission basis but receive a draw if they are unable to produce sufficient commissions to match the draw, they may have to return

- In order to survive at a new firm, the account executive looks to former clients and tries to take business from the prior firm.

This system encourages bad selection of people to enter the insurance field. A seasoned underwriter who wants to get into the agency ranks will certainly not be able to do so without a paycheck for a long period of time.

This system also creates bad selection of clients. A commissioned salesperson is typically going to bring in any client they can find if they can sell them on going for the lowest price.

Another example of efficiency gone wrong is an insurance agent's use of form letters. Everyone knows when a form letter is being used, and it creates the perception that the client is not especially important to the writer.

Consultants can help you figure out which agents have more hat than cattle. There are advantages of using such independent property and casualty insurance advisers:

- You will have an independent review of the proposals by an expert in property and casualty insurance.
- The insurance adviser will allow you to borrow expertise that you are unlikely to have.
- The adviser will have no allegiance to any insurance carrier or insurance agent and will not be paid on a commission basis.
- The adviser can recommend coverages that you may not have and that may not have been considered by the proposing agents.
- The adviser can recommend coverages that can be deleted or modified and that may reduce your insurance costs.
- The adviser can assess the expertise of the competing agents.

- Once a decision has been made, the policies, when issued, can be reviewed to determine if they represent what was promised.
- The integrity of the insurance carriers can be assessed from a financial standpoint.
- This person can be a resource throughout the policy year.

The cost of an independent adviser on property and casualty insurance is based on time expended and the scope of the engagement, and to a large degree, it depends on where you are at in the insurance-buying process.

For example, if you have several quotes in hand that need to be reviewed and your insurance expiration date is several days away, an insurance adviser can quickly look at the proposals and give you an opinion.

The adviser can also get involved at the beginning of the process by assessing what you have and what you need. The adviser can work with agents you choose to answer questions and to provide information needed to quote.

It's time to expect more cattle than hat from your agent, just as you would your doctor, your CPA, your financial adviser, or your lawyer. Your business is worth it.

10

The Insurance Audition

It's time to give your agent, or the agent proposing on your business insurance, a stress test.

When you go to the cardiologist, he or she gives you a stress test to see how well your heart measures up under stressful physical conditions. It is an early diagnostic approach for assessing the risk of a potentially deadly heart attack.

We need these kinds of tests in the insurance business in the form of auditions or casting calls.

The typical arrangement in buying business insurance is inherently flawed. Here is how it typically works.

Every year or so, you allow five agencies to bid your company's property and casualty business insurance. You meet with the agents and give them a copy of all current policies and ask them to quote exactly what the company currently has, apples to apples.

The agents prepare applications, answering important questions about your account for various insurance carriers. You never see these applications, although under Michigan law you are typically bound by how they are answered.

The multiple insurance carriers that the agents are quoting ask to visit your locations to inspect your facilities. (Five insurance agents asking for bids from three different insurance carriers is equal to fifteen visits of at least one hour each.) These agents ultimately bring you multiple quotations from multiple insurance companies in various formats.

You make a selection based on the lowest premium, not being skilled in the art of understanding the terms and conditions of the various insurance policies being proposed and, in many cases, not having been given sample policy language to review. Even if you are given sample policies, it is virtually impossible for a layperson to compare policy language differences and to understand what endorsement options are available.

The policies are delivered, with or without a summary of insurance from the agent. They are filed, and the process goes on, year after year.

The insurance agent receives a commission and puts the file away until the insurance buyer calls to ask for changes, such as automobile changes, or to make a claim.

The problem with the above process is that it is very time-consuming, tends to favor price over quality, and causes agents to run into one another in the marketplace. Unlike health insurance, property and casualty insurance agents are normally held to the rule of "one insurer / one agent," and thus, once an agent has sent in an application to an insurer, that market is blocked and cannot be used by other agents.

Would you shop your doctor by saying he or she could only access certain hospitals and other medical resources because your other doctors had already blocked those sources of care? Of course not. Instead most would pick the doctor they feel most comfortable with to be the quarterback of their health.

One solution is to hold an insurance audition where prospective insurance agents, as well as the incumbent agent, are separately interviewed and evaluated, with one agency being selected to be the quarterback of marketing your account with the multitude of insurers.

We believe the concept of an audition before the selection is a good method of finding out what will happen *after* you select a firm to be your risk manager and insurance buyer. The insurance audition is at no cost to you and will likely provide you, as the buyer, with valuable information on the market and coverage options.

We would encourage you to also make time for your candidates to meet with you and other management people so the candidates can learn as much as possible about your company. At this meeting, no sales pitch or quotations should be allowed.

The first step is to select candidates from one or more firms, including your current agent. Because your current agent has been your agent and presumably your risk manager, they have already auditioned, and you may want to skip that agency for this part of the process.

The second step is to provide the agencies all the information and research time they request.

The third step is to ask the agents that you have chosen to prepare a report of recommendations and to make their case about the qualifications and experience of the person or persons who will be providing services on your account and what they would recommend for your insurance and risk management program.

Premiums should not be quoted, and applications should not be submitted to any insurance carrier as of this point.

Based on these reports, pick the agent that most impresses you based on the work that has been done. Ask them to come in and make a presentation and answer any questions that you may have. You can then ask the selected agent to send applications to various insurance carriers so that a fully negotiated insurance and risk management program can be presented to you. This should be done at least thirty

(30) days before the effective date of your renewal so that there will be time to make changes in the proposed program well before the renewal date.

There is one caveat in all this: If you are not willing to consider firing your current agent when another firm is better, do not go through this process. If the competing firms end up being clearly better than what you have now but you are unable to make the change, you will end up burning out the agent-broker insurance market. And if you decide to make a change in the future, they may not be available to you.

The goal is to secure the services of a professional insurance buyer and a professional risk manager. The entity that is selected will then go into the marketplace and secure quotations and be able to compare terms and conditions and make a recommendation to you based on all factors. That same firm will provide all this in consideration of the commissions that are paid by insurance carriers, or they may want a fee in addition to commissions.

At a minimum, you should expect an insightful analysis of your current policies and risk management program, including

- the good and the bad terms and conditions of your current insurance policies;
- an analysis of your claims history and recommendations;
- a review of the "risk of loss" provisions of your lease (if applicable) and customer agreements, as well as independent contractor agreements and temporary employment or contract labor agreements;
- crime loss recommendations;
- cyber loss recommendations;
- recommendations on insurance carriers suited to your account; and
- an analysis of terms and conditions of competing insurance carriers.

Some believe that having more than one broker can help keep the others honest. There are other ways to do that, including retaining an outside consultant to keep them on their toes.

A related issue is that many commercial insurance buyers do not know how to audition brokers. We typically look to the following points of consideration:

- Length of experience in insurance.
- Specialty in particular industries.
- Will the agency/agent send you a letter confirming the existence of more than an order-taker relationship?
- Does the agent have a system of passing the account off after the sale is made? (This may be hard to judge because most agents will claim they have an ongoing involvement in the account when in reality it is the CSR you will be working with most of the time.)
- What advanced insurance industry designations has the agent obtained? (If they have none, it sends the message that the selling price may be more important to them.)
- Ask the agent to take your current policies and to come back with a report on any deficiencies or suggestions. If you have multiple entities, see if their report includes mention of how those should be covered under the various policies.
- Ask a consultant who regularly compares agencies to assist you in the auditioning.
- Ask your attorney to sit in on the interviews.

Want a sobriety check on your knowledge of business insurance? Take the true-or-false quiz at www.packingyourparachute.com. Better yet, have the competing agents take it.

11

Venial and Mortal Sins in Insurance

Sins of the insurance buyer can be venial (minor) or mortal (grave). Usually, even duct tape cannot fix the mortal ones.

Examples of venial, minor sins in business insurance are

- not buying broad-form collision coverage,
- not buying higher limits for off-premises power failure,
- having a $250 deductible for collision coverage when you should have $1,000,
- turning in small claims,
- failing to maintain an ERISA bond,
- not having a broad-form notice of occurrence endorsement on your general liability policy, and
- not having a blanket-named insured endorsement and additional insured endorsement on your general liability policy.

Examples of mortal, grave sins in business insurance are

- hiring an agent who is an order-taker and who does not provide advice or suggestions;
- failing to list all entity names from your organization on all policies;
- failing to give copies of lease agreements to your insurance agent;

- having a protective safeguards warranty endorsement on your property insurance, which bars coverage if you did not have a fire sprinkler system, burglar alarm, fire alarm, or certain kinds of outside lighting;
- having too-low limits for building or contents and failing to have blanket limits instead of separate limits by location;
- allowing a coinsurance penalty provision on any aspect of your property insurance;
- not expanding business interruption coverage to beyond thirty days after your building is rebuilt;
- allowing your insurance agent to complete your applications; and
- buying insurance on the Internet.

Businesses obviously want to look carefully at all aspects of insurance but should start from the premise that the mortal sins are nonnegotiable, except in situations where the coverage is unavailable due to loss history or other underwriting reasons.

Here are ten real-life examples of cases we have been involved in that turned out to be mortal sins in buying insurance. The names have been changed to protect the parties. Of course, this list is not exhaustive.

1. **Mortal sin: Buying insurance on the Internet**

    McGeorge. Mr. McGeorge leased a new car. In the process, he went online to buy auto insurance from a major national insurer. Unknowingly, he selected basic collision, which, while cheaper, gave him no coverage for collision if his vehicle were damaged in an accident that was his fault.

    As luck would have it, he slid on ice a few weeks later, totaling his vehicle. Ultimately, he was unable to pay the loan because he had to secure another vehicle and loan, and Ford sued him.

    In today's online marketplace, the ability for consumers to purchase insurance over the Internet is greater than ever.

With the continued development of electronic security and online bill payment, online insurance transactions are becoming more and more common.

In 2007, the greatest growth in online insurance purchases was for personal auto policies. Some studies show that more than 30 percent of auto insurance sales will take place online by 2017, compared with 10 percent of individual life insurance sales and over 50 percent of individual health insurance sales.

Despite the latest trends, consumers might want to consider the following pitfalls before committing to an online insurance program.

The most obvious problem with online insurance policies is the lack of a physical infrastructure. In most cases, online insurance companies maintain their operations at a national headquarters or a call center. This means that most policyholders can only communicate with their insurance company via Internet or telephone. In the event of a catastrophe or other major loss, it may not be possible to communicate with your insurance carrier for an extended period of time.

Independent agents, on the other hand, offer a local presence that is unmatched by any online website. This allows the agent to personally respond to any emergency claims or simply meet with the policyholder face-to-face to discuss policy changes. Also, independent agents are usually authorized to accept last-minute payments from the policyholder in order to prevent policy cancellation. Some online insurance carriers are limited in their ability to accept overdue payments and, in some circumstances, may even charge a transaction fee.

One of the most unknown facts about the online insurance industry involves the use of underwriting companies. These are companies within the main insurance company that are under common ownership or control and that sell insurance in a specific state. Collectively, these entities are the "family of companies" and are operated under the main insurance company brand. The details of these entities are usually found in the fine print of the terms and conditions for use of the website. For example, assume an insurance buyer purchases a policy from the acme.com insurance company. Even though the policy carries the acme.com logo, the actual coverages are provided through XYZ Insurance Company as the underwriting company.

The reason that online insurance carriers create state-specific underwriting companies is that it allows the carrier to deny or limit losses for certain out-of-state claims. As long as the insurer maintains separate underwriting companies and does not file certificates in any other states, that insurer might be able to avoid out-of-state liability.

For example, if an Ohio resident was injured in Michigan, the Ohio insurance carrier is only obligated to pay for Michigan benefits if that insurance company had filed its certificate with the Michigan OFIS. The savvy insurance company will avoid this at all costs.

An independent insurance agent is more likely to review an insured's list of assets, do in-home visits, and offer advice for what types of insurance to buy. Insurance agents also make themselves available for updates and insurance policy reviews. Compare this to buying an online insurance policy where customers are more than likely to be pushed to the insurance company's customer service department or national call center where they will be one of a million or more customers.

In the online arrangement, policy reviews and updates are usually based on call center scripts using boilerplate language or a series of predetermined questions. These scripts may have very little to do with the insured's insurance program and ever-changing exposures.

Most policyholders rely on their insurance agents to provide much-needed expertise on technical insurance issues. In fact, many independent agents strive to develop a personal and long-term relationship with each of their policyholders. This allows the agent to ask pertinent questions about exposures and anticipate the need for policy changes. Ultimately, this close relationship allows the insurance agent to better understand the nature of the policyholder's exposures.

With most online insurance companies, policyholders are left to figure the coverages out for themselves, both before and after the loss. As a consumer navigates an online insurance quote, he or she must select a number of different coverages and limits. Absent a background in insurance, it is unlikely that the average consumer would fully understand these coverages or the adequacy of the limits.

Most online insurance carriers are structured in such a way that no special relationship could possibly exist. This limits the liability of the insurance carrier for suits alleging that its staff failed to advise the policyholder of the proper coverages.

Another point to consider is that most online carriers require that the policyholder release the company from liability arising out of the use of their website. This means that if you inadvertently enter the wrong policy limit from a drop-down box because the website layout was confusing, you cannot sue the insurance carrier. In the same way, if the carrier inadvertently publishes your social security or credit card number, you may be barred from bringing a suit.

Without extensive insurance knowledge, buying online insurance can be confusing. Special limits, exclusions, no-fault coverage, broad-form collision coverage, and mini-tort protection are important terms to know and may not be fully explained in an online insurance quote. Without the input of a licensed insurance agent, consumers are left to their own devices when they try to get insurance estimates online.

Online customer service representatives (CSR) are mere order-takers and are not always required to be licensed as insurance agents by the state's department of insurance. Moreover, online CSRs are usually trained in-house by their employer and oftentimes lack the experience or expertise in other areas of insurance.

2. **Mortal sin: Relying upon a certificate of insurance when there was no coverage, resulting in the personal bankruptcy of the business and the owner of the business**

GMO Operating. In this 2014 case, an insurance agency issued a certificate of property insurance for a chemical manufacturer, but coverage was not actually in force and was never placed. Following a fire, it was revealed that there was no coverage. The insured business could not recover, and it closed. Its lawsuit against the insurance agency lasted more than two years, while the insured owner filed for personal bankruptcy.

3. **Mortal sin: Not insuring enough for the replacement cost of buildings and/or business personal property**

Jake's Bakery. A bakery was destroyed by fire in 2012. The account had been referred to a service center that relied on an inflation guard provision and did not properly assess the values. The insured had relied on the agent to determine the value of the building and contents. The proceeds received from the building insurer were substantially less than the amount of the loss. The insured went out of business.

Prototype Inc. In this 2014 case, a fire occurred to a building where the ultimate damages were determined to be $5,239,041 for the building and $1,170,052 for business-personal property. The limits purchased were $1,400,000 for the building and $252,000 for the contents. The owner testified that she relied on the insurance agent to set and advise the limits of the policy and to secure replacement cost coverage. The court disagreed, finding no evidence of a breach of duty of loyalty and good faith.

4. **Mortal sin: Failing to have adequate automobile liability insurance limits**

   McBridge. The sixteen-year-old daughter of a wealthy father was involved in a serious automobile accident in his vehicle. The vehicle was only insured for $100,000 in liability coverage, and the owner had no personal umbrella policy.

   We find that many policyholders think that they can only be sued up to their policy limit for liability insurance. This is not true. The plaintiff's attorneys have an ethical obligation to seek the full amount of the damages sustained by the plaintiff. It would be a violation of the rules of professional conduct for an attorney to intentionally limit their client's recovery to the limits available under the defendant's insurance coverage. If attorneys only demanded damages in an amount that was insured, there would be no claims against uninsured individuals. This clearly goes against public policy.

   Assuming, for example, that $250,000 of a $1,000,000 judgment is covered by insurance, the plaintiff's attorney will attempt to garnish or otherwise execute against all other assets owned by the defendant to satisfy the uncollected portion.

   There is also a misconception that civil judgments can only be collected for up to ten years, after which time the judgment is dissolved. This is not true. In many states, civil judgments are valid for up to ten years but are renewable in ten-year increments, *indefinitely.*

5. **Mortal sin: Not having adequate limits for ordinance or law coverage**

   ABC Church. In this 2012 case, a church in a suburban area suffered a major fire loss. After the loss, the city required that the church be rebuilt in a more expensive manner—to the extent of $750,000 in additional costs—to install more expensive beams and to otherwise bring the building up to code. It was determined that there was only $50,000 in ordinance or law coverage.

6. **Mortal sin: Letting someone else insure your property**

Ethan Properties LLC. In this circuit court case, the building owned by the insured was insured by a land contractor vendee. The seller was listed as a "loss payee" only. Following a major fire, the insurer denied coverage to all parties, stating that the named insured vendee engaged in misconduct, voiding coverage.

7. **Mortal sin: Not asking for coverage for a co-lessee of a motor vehicle**

Frank. Mr. Frank co-leased a vehicle with his mother. He was involved in a collision and suffered serious injuries. He and his mother used the vehicle to provide care for an ill family member. Frank, who did not live with his mother, was not disclosed as a driver or named as an insured on his mother's auto policy. After coverage was denied by the insurer, Frank sued his agent. The case was dismissed after a finding that there was no duty to list Frank as an insured, even if the agent knew about the co-lessee status.

8. **Mortal sin: Not reviewing and signing applications for insurance to assure correct information**

Market Village. In this 2013 case, the insurer denied coverage for a fire loss to a large grocery store, citing certain misstatements in the application, which was completed by the insurance agent, including the age of the building. Extensive litigation resulted.

9. **Mortal sin: Not having business interruption coverage for property in transit or at other locations**

   Restoration service. A restoration company provided portable document freeze-drying services for businesses that suffered water losses. After a fire that damaged one of the expensive portable units, the company could not perform jobs and lost income and incurred extra expenses for which it was not covered. It sued its agent, which cost it thousands of dollars.

10. **Mortal sin: Not addressing vacancy provisions in commercial property insurance policies**

    Water Mountain Complex. After vandalism to a vacant ice arena, the insurer denied coverage, stating the building had been vacant more than sixty days. The insured had to sue its insurance agent, who denied liability, stating that they had no duty to advise on anything as they were an order-taker.

12

Autocorrect Can Go Straight to He'll

Don't rely on an autocorrect feature to somehow straighten out an incorrectly packed parachute. There is nothing built into the product to tell you it was folded wrong and may not open. It's not going to beep at you to alert you to the possibility that you won't be getting the protection you think you are getting and might just free-fall.

Even where the product is a bunch of words, i.e. an insurance policy, the computer does not adjust to what it thinks you meant to purchase or should have purchased. It only issues the policy as it was requested to by the insurance agent.

Business insurance is just like a parachute jump. You want to get it right the first time. It may well be too late to even get a second jump.

Miss a name? Don't expect that it will be automatically added. Leave off a location? Shocker—the system won't pull the address from a database and include it. It's just the way it is in this business.

Over the past forty-one years as insurance coverage attorneys, expert witnesses in property insurance claims, and insurance agents, we have seen many insureds who had autocorrect expectations when dealing with insurers and insurance agents. Here are our top ten favorites:

Autocorrect myth no. 1. If an entity named is not listed, the insurer will just add it later.

Autocorrect myth no. 2. By using the word *any* in my insurance policy exclusions and conditions, the insurer does not mean *any*. Next time you read your insurance policy, take a look at how many times the word *any* is used. Here are a few examples:

> "Any earth movement"
> "Any pollutant"
> "Any insured"
> "Any statute"
> "Any person"
> "Any premises"
> "Any contractors"
> "Any auto"
> "Any part of it"
> "Any manner"
> "Any of the other insurance"
> "Any good or products"

Autocorrect myth no. 3. If your fire sprinkler system works at least partially, the insurer will not enforce the protective safeguards clause and pay the claim because the underwriter said it was only intended to apply if we shut off the system or did not have one.

Autocorrect myth no. 4. After a fire, if we find that we did not insure enough, this can be rectified so that we won't have a problem with the coinsurance penalty provision.

Autocorrect myth no. 5. After a major property loss, our customers will understand and not enforce a penalty for our inability to perform on time. If not, our insurer will autocorrect this because it is a business interruption.

Autocorrect myth no. 6. If there are not enough insurance limits on the building, the insurer will find a way to correct this in rebuilding the building because we have replacement cost coverage.

Autocorrect myth no. 7. Although we have a monthly limit on our business interruption coverage, the insurer can fix this by rolling over what we did use in the prior month.

Autocorrect myth no. 8. My insurer will correct the debris removal limit to clean up the property because otherwise we won't be able to rebuild the building.

Autocorrect myth no. 9. Our insurer will correct our coverage for loss of income until we are totally up to speed following a loss because they want us to get back to where we were before the loss. That's the purpose of insurance.

Autocorrect myth no. 10. If the building codes require us to rebuild with a setback, the insurer will help us correct this by finding another location so that we do not have this problem to deal with.

13

Sticks and Stones Can Break Bones, but Names *Will* Also Hurt

There is an epidemic in the insurance industry that relates to missing or inaccurately listed entity names on the policies' schedules of named insureds, additional insureds, or loss payees.

One might think that when an entity name such as an LLC is not listed on a policy as an insured, this "oversight" might be overlooked by the insurer as a simple mistake. Our experiences suggest that in most cases, you should not expect forgiveness from the insurance company adjuster if this happens to you.

Adjusters are charged with the responsibility of systematically evaluating each claim as it comes in, with the first order of business being whether the name of the entity seeking coverage is covered as an insured. It amazes us in our review of hundreds of insurance programs that missing names are as common as words are to a dictionary. This is often the result of either an insurance agent not asking the right questions or improperly listing names on the policy.

We also see a great deal of inconsistency between how names are listed among various policies, i.e. property insurance, liability insurance, workers' compensation, automobile, etc.

Do yourself a favor—*require* that your agent do a named insured grid that lists all the names on the vertical column and all the policies on the horizontal column. It may be enlightening to you which entities are covered and which are not. It may also make you consider adding some that may be missing.

And another thing—consider how names are listed, i.e. first named insured? Named insured? An insured? Additional insured? Loss payee? Lenders loss payable? All insured parties are not created equally.

The totem pole of those covered on commercial general liability insurance policies goes something like this:

First named insured. This is the party that must pay the premium and is the only name that can make coverage changes.

Other named insureds. These are commonly owned entities that are also listed as the named insureds and should not be listed as additional insureds.

Insureds. Most policies grant coverage automatically to certain groups like employees of the named insured, shareholders, etc.

Additional insureds. These are companies that are indirectly related to the named insured(s) that want to be listed on your liability insurance. Examples of this are landlords wanting to be listed on the tenant's CGL policy or the owner of property wanting to be listed as an additional insured on the subcontractor's policy.

Importantly, these additional insureds do not have independent coverage. If they are sued for their own negligence, which is unrelated to the named insured, they would not be covered. Thus, do not rely on being an additional insured on someone else's liability policy. Be sure to have your own.

There is often similar confusion with how parties are covered under property insurance policies.

Loss payees. They are inferior parties listed on a property insurance policy. These parties have no independent rights. If the named insured torches the building, the loss payee is also out of luck.

We routinely see building owners who allow tenants under a triple-net lease to insure their property to be listed as loss payees. Good luck if the tenant voids the policy through a misstatement on an application or intentional conduct such as arson. The owner would have no coverage.

Mortgagee. Holders of secured interests in real estate are listed as mortgagees on the borrower's policy.

Lenders loss payable. These parties are listed because they have a lien or other interest in the equipment or personal property of the named insured, i.e. a bank that loaned money.

The problem of missing or inaccurately listed insureds is at epidemic proportions with the relative ease of the formation of limited liability companies, which now exceed corporations in number in many states, and with many joint ventures in the global economy.

Many insurance agents will not ask about all entity names and will rely on what the company's main name is. This is a mistake that could lead to disaster.

Here are some tips on the listing of names:

1. **Many insurance agents do not think to add building owner names, such as LLCs, to business auto policies, leaving such entities with major assets fully uncovered.**

    Some exposures in this area include an employee driving to a real-estate closing or a parking lot accident where a janitor drives into a tenant who is leaving the building. Motor vehicle leases and titles should be examined to ascertain what the correct entity name is, as we often find inconsistencies in this area.

2. **In most cases, liquor liability policies do not automatically list the landlord as an additional insured.** If there are any liquor sales in a building you own, be sure to ask for this endorsement from your tenant's liquor liability insurer.

3. **Where the building owner requires the tenant to insure the building for fires and other losses, we often do not see the landlord entity listed on that policy, and where we do, many times the listing is improper.**

   If the landlord is listed as a loss payee on the tenant's policy that insures the building, this is unacceptable, as the landlord would have no independent rights to coverage. In short, if the tenant commits arson, the landlord as a loss payee has no coverage. In this situation, the landlord should be listed as an additional insured on the property insurance purchased by the tenant.

4. **Assumed names create weighty issues.**

   Where a company files an assumed name and the named insured is listed as "ABC Corporation DBA: Joe's Consulting," for example, note that only Joe's Consulting would be covered and other acts of the corporation not doing business as that name may be uncovered. It is best to list the corporation entity name and then *also* separately list the DBAs.

5. **Insist that entity names are fully listed.**

   For example, if the name of the company is ABC Manufacturing Inc., be certain that the *Inc.* is listed. The same applies to limited liability companies, partnerships, and joint ventures. The reason for this is that many insurance policies extend ancillary coverages for shareholders, members, partners, etc., depending on the type of named insured listed.

6. **Nonemploying entities should usually still be listed on workers' compensation policies.**

   The reason for this is issue of uninsured independent contractors.

   For example, where you hire a contractor to do repairs at your building, an injury to the contractor's employee could result in a workers' compensation claim against you if the contractor was not insured.

7. **Try to add 401(k) plan entity names as named insureds on your general liability policy.**

   Most insurers will add such entity names for no charge. Of course, separate fiduciary liability coverage should also be maintained for ERISA claims.

8. **Be cautious who you list as the first of the named insureds.**

   Although it is possible to have many entities listed as named insureds, which is the broadest protection for an entity, the entity listed first is the "captain" of all the insureds and is the only one who can make coverage changes and effectuate cancellations and bears the sole responsibility for paying the premiums. Carefully consider who that entity should be.

9. **Look at who owns or leases the motor vehicle and compare that to what coverages apply.**

   We find many vehicles owned or leased in the company name that are insured in the personal name of the officer. This leaves the company potentially open to uncovered liability. If a vehicle is leased by the corporation, for example, and not insured on the business automobile policy but instead on the personal auto policy without the corporation being added as an additional insured, this could create a coverage problem.

Moreover, the liability limits are an issue because many personal umbrellas will not extend coverage to a business entity even if listed on the primary automobile policy, and this could ultimately expose the business entity to major underinsurance. The general rule that should be followed is that every entity should insure its own exposures even if the business is owned by the same person that is the named insured on a personal auto policy.

10. **Carefully consider automatic "blanket" or additional insured endorsements.**

Leases often specify that the landlord is to be listed as an additional insured. However, automatic landlord additional insured language found on most general liability insurance policies may not provide as broad of a protection as you might think. For example, most policies that provide automatic additional insured coverage to landlords also exclude coverage for renovations, and there are other limitations that apply. Landlords should also always maintain their own independent general liability insurance policy and umbrella policy, which list the landlord entity as a named insured.

11. **Past partnerships and joint ventures are not automatically covered under general liability policies**.

In fact, you should assume that you have no coverage for any name not listed as a named insured.

Sloppiness appears to be the norm rather than the exception among many insurance agents when it comes to how names are listed and whether such names are consistently listed between policies. A simple named insured grid can easily expose gaps that might be addressed before a loss. For a sample, go to www.packingyourparachute.com.

14

Due to Budget Cuts, the Light at the End of the Tunnel Is Now Off

You can save me 20 percent off my insurance bill? Funny, how do you know that when you don't know what I am paying or what my loss history is?

What if the following happened?

- A doctor said that he/she would treat you the same way your current physician treats you but for 20 percent less in co-pays and deductibles?
- The independent storefront tax preparer service using part-time workers to do tax returns said that they wanted to expand their services and be your tax adviser and they would do it for 20 percent less in fees?
- A recent law school graduate wants to defend you in a major lawsuit and claims it would be 20 percent less in legal fees than the big firms?
- A solicitor is in your lobby and claims to be newly licensed as an insurance agent after taking a forty-hour class and states that he/she can save you 20 percent on your current insurance premiums and wants to have a copy of your current insurance policies and premiums?

It seems sometimes that spreadsheets that measure percentage savings were invented for the insurance industry. We see them routinely used by buyers in comparing pricing by policy type. This is what we call spreadsheet silhouettes because of the inability to really compare what is being purchased.

We often find that the big picture of insurance protection is overlooked. The seesaw of the lowest price is often the winner, at least in the short term. Yet it is the quality and design of the insurance and risk management program that might well be the light at the end of the tunnel following a disaster.

For a spreadsheet checklist comparison to be of any real value, the reviewer must be able to decipher key information on coverages and include that in the line-item version. This is generally a tall order for most inexperienced insurance buyers or even some insurance agents and might only be effective where prepared by an insurance consultant or other experienced professional.

Liberty is one of the largest writers of insurance in the United States. The president of Liberty, Tim Rose, was quoted as saying,

> I'm beginning to feel that risks that shop every year for rate decreases are starting to be viewed negatively by the underwriting community. We're doing that, and we've seen some evidence of others doing that too.

Executives burn out the market when they shop the business insurance based on price because there are fewer carriers in the business than in prior years. Mergers, consolidations, and technology have made it easier to know the history of the buyers, and believe us, insurers keep track.

There is no patience with insurance carriers in quoting accounts repeatedly and not getting the business. The underwriters are simply spread too thin. It is expensive for an insurance carrier to inspect a prospect's locations, underwrite the data, and provide a proposal. When it does not get the business, this is noted in their computer system, potentially affecting the account for future consideration with that insurer.

If you feel the need to shop insurance, you need to examine what you are trying to accomplish. If it is to secure better terms and conditions or to obtain better claims handling, this may be a worthy endeavor. If it is to reduce your insurance costs without understanding the terms and conditions or risks involved, this process should be reconsidered.

Beware of the spreadsheet silhouette.

15

Dancing the Foxtrot while Your Professionals Are Doing the Rumba

Insurance cannot be purchased in a vacuum. To do it properly, business insurance programs must be developed by a team of both internal personnel, such as chief financial officers, chief operating officers, and production managers, and outside professionals, such as CPAs, attorneys, and coverage consultants.

Here is an example:

Administrative actions such as Equal Opportunity Employment Commission (EEOC) or Department of Labor investigations are usually either handled internally by the insured's human resources department or by its outside law firm. When this happens, the company may be voiding its employment practices liability coverage for failure to provide the insurer notice of a potential claim. When the EEOC dismisses the matter and the former employee then files suit in court, the company may be in for a surprise.

Outside accountants and CPAs are a wealth of information on your risks and exposures. They are not often included in insurance renewal discussions but should be. For example, they likely have specific knowledge of the business interruption limits that are needed, as well as the value of assets.

Appraisers of real and personal property, as well as contractors, can be helpful in establishing values and evaluating building code updates that might be needed.

Temporary staffing businesses that supply workers to your company should also be considered for what they add to the overall insurance risks presented to your company.

16

A World without Insurance

The word *insurance* was used 513 times in this book. Not surprising, given that this is a book suggesting a new way to buy it.

But what if the government passed a law that prohibited the purchase of insurance to cover your personal or business assets?

You as a business person would have to absorb and pay for any losses resulting from damage to your buildings, personal property, or business interruption, as well as any liability claims that may be made against you because of injury on your premises, either to third parties or to your employees, and so forth.

- Would you look at risk of loss any differently?
- Would you seek advice to help you prevent losses?
- Would you listen to that advice?
- Would you begin to reconsider risks such as
    - risky drivers,
    - uninsured subcontractors,
    - bad hold harmless agreements,
    - bad indemnity agreements,
    - inappropriate employment practices,
    - inadequate fire protection systems,
    - bad lease agreements, or
    - temporary employment arrangements?

Recently, a sprinkler contractor made a recommendation to its client to either upgrade its fire sprinkler system or reduce the stacking of inventory in the plant. That contractor indicated that in the event of a fire, the sprinkler system would not be able to suppress the fire. The client had the option of complying with this recommendation or assuming the risk of a total loss. With insurance, a typical insured would fight this or delay its implementation. Without insurance, the decision might be different.

Sometimes the best way to protect your business does not involve paying a premium.

It is an interesting fact that of the $13,000,000–$16,000,000 in liability claims filed by the *Titanic* passengers and their families, only $64,000 was paid out by the shipping company and its insurers. One of the defenses was the clause within the passenger tickets that absolved the ship company of liability.[12]

Our long-standing belief is that sometimes non–insurance risk management can be even more powerful than buying insurance, although a business should almost always do both.

Disclaimers and limitations of liability provisions in purchase agreements, construction agreements, product sales agreements, websites, and leases can be extremely effective, just as it appears to have been in the *Titanic* ticket language.

In the technological day and age, many of these disclaimers are activated through online clicks where terms and conditions are accepted, most of the time without them being read. These can include limitations of liability, disclaimer of consequential damages, waivers of subrogation, and arbitration provisions.

Another very effective risk management tool is the transfer of your risk in a contract you enter into with another company, such as a tenant or subcontractor. This risk management technique is very powerful in that it requires the assuming party (the indemnitor) to defend, indemnify, and hold your company and sometimes its representatives harmless from certain suits, demands, or claims.

A common scenario is the assumption of risk in a lease agreement. In an indemnification provision in a lease, the landlord will typically attempt to require the tenant to indemnify and hold it harmless of and from "any" liability for injuries "on or about" the demised premises. The words in quotes are very broad in scope. If a third party visiting the premises gets hurt in the parking lot and sues the landlord, does the tenant have to indemnify the landlord for that? Depending on the indemnification language, it certainly could.

Many attorneys think that if the tenant's liability insurance policy includes $1,000,000 coverage for "property damage," this means that if the landlord or its insurer sues the tenant for accidentally starting a fire that damages the leased space, the tenant should have $1,000,000 in coverage. Almost always this will not be so given that most such policies have a sublimit for liability for damage to property in the care, custody, or control of the tenant. A waiver of subrogation in the lease agreement should be negotiated as a non–insurance risk management measure to block such claims by the respective insurers.

Other issues include overbroad repair clauses requiring the tenant to repair the building even if there is a casualty that is insured by the landlord's property policy.

Perhaps the biggest mistake of a landlord (or any party for that matter) is to allow the tenant or anyone else to insure its property. We often see so-called triple-net leases where the tenant agrees to insure the building. These should be outlawed. They expose the landlord and the tenant to major loss and liability.

Would you let someone outside your family insure your house? Your car? Probably not. Why? You know your exposures and property better than someone else, and you would not want to rely on that other person or their insurance agent who you probably have never even met.

Businesses should not only carefully review the precise language of agreements where other parties have agreed to indemnify it but should also confirm that the insurance coverage backing up such indemnification provisions exists with adequate limits.

Correspondingly, businesses should look to see what coverage they have for liability of others they assume in contracts. Not all insurance coverages are alike in this area. Most insurance companies will only cover liability assumed in an indemnification agreement for "bodily injury" and "property damage." There are endorsements available that can broaden this to include assumed liability pertaining to libel, slander, defamation, and other non–bodily injury claims. Some other carriers will add a contractual liability limitation that can significantly limit or remove coverage for such indemnification provisions. Such limitations are dangerous.

As to intellectual property liability claims of violation of copyright, trademark, and patent, coverage is typically nonexistent, and this should be carefully considered from a risk management standpoint. For example, if services your business provides to another company are determined to violate a copyright or trademark, there is usually no coverage not only for the direct liability of your business but also for any liability you have assumed in an agreement with your customer.

A similar problem exists as to assuming liability for cyber-related incidents, even if you have purchased a cyber policy. The reason for this is that most such cyber policies exclude contractually assumed liability.

For a list of items to consider in insurance and indemnity provisions, whether from the perspective of the company transferring or assuming the risks, visit www.packingyourparachute.com.

17

A Stick and a Begging Purse

There is an old maxim that all people have both a stick and a begging purse—a stick when we have the leverage in a negotiation and a begging purse when we don't.

In the business of buying insurance, some accounts have more options than others. This often depends on the nature of the business, the state of the insurance market, trends in insurance, loss history, the strength of management and financials, attitudes toward risk, and other factors.

The trick in buying insurance is to be able to use your stick more than your begging purse. This is done through a comprehensive approach to risk management, including loss control, safety committees, risk transfer, strong management, cooperation with insurance company requests, and not shopping the insurance every year. In short, you need to present your company as highly desirable. This will help your professionals negotiate the better-than-average coverages and pricing.

Overshopping insurance when you have more of a begging purse than a stick has many disadvantages, not least of which is that the frequent request for quotes from the insurance carrier will soon get that account placed on the insurance carriers "no quote" list.

The point to effectively buying business insurance is to make your parachute and backpack as desirable as possible—one that your professionals and insurers want to be part of packing with you and your team. In doing so, you can negotiate better terms and pricing and get noticed by insurers and insurance agencies that you might not otherwise.

18

The Policyholder's Bill of Rights

In May of 2016, the Republic of the Philippines' Insurance Commission issued the Bill of Rights of Policyholders to enumerate the basic rights of its country's insureds under its Insurance Code.[13]

In the US, astonishingly, not all states have such a policyholder bill of rights.

Florida's bill provides standards for its insurance department in exercising its powers and duties and in adopting rules.[14] It provides the following:

a. Policyholders shall have the right to competitive pricing practices and marketing methods that enable them to determine the best value among comparable policies.
b. Policyholders shall have the right to obtain comprehensive coverage.
c. Policyholders shall have the right to insurance advertising and other selling approaches that provide accurate and balanced information on the benefits and limitations of a policy.
d. Policyholders shall have a right to an insurance company that is financially stable.
e. Policyholders shall have the right to be serviced by a competent, honest insurance agent or broker.

f. Policyholders shall have the right to a readable policy.
g. Policyholders shall have the right to an insurance company that provides an economic delivery of coverage and that tries to prevent losses.
h. Policyholders shall have the right to a balanced and positive regulation by the department, commission, and office.

Alabama, Louisiana, and Texas have similar statutes providing somewhat similar requirements.[15]

Mississippi has a statute called the Mississippi Homeowner Insurance Policyholder Bill of Rights.[16]

The Michigan Insurance Code requires that a written notice be provided to the policyholder concerning rates[17] but has no other such statute called a policyholder's bill of rights.

All states should have a *business owner* policyholder's bill of rights that is posted on the website of the state's insurance department and is included with all policies like in Texas, which requires that a copy of the Bill of Rights be included with all issued policies.

While a policyholder bill of rights does not generally provide for a private cause of action against an insurer for a violation, it sets the stage for a more balanced playing field.

Here is what we think should be in a policyholder's bill of rights:

1. The right to get a complete copy of the policy before purchasing the coverage
2. The right to rely on the statements of an insurance agent appointed by an insurer and to have those statements be binding upon that insurer
3. The right to not be discriminated against if you use a public adjuster to assist in adjusting an insurance claim

4. The right to request that an insurance agent inform you of the nature of the business relationship and that, if the agent desires to only be order-takers, this be communicated in writing
5. The right to have the insurance company cooperate with you as the insured in the adjustment of the claim just as you are obligated to cooperate with it

19

A Different Kettle of Fish

It's time for a different kettle of fish in buying business insurance.

A culture of packing your business parachute where good service is defined more by the integrity of the insurance program and less by the glossy brochure or how quickly the e-mail or phone call is returned.

A different level of expectations of insurance agents where it is more about cattle and less about hat.

A different manner of the buyer viewing risk and insurance as other than a bystander.

A different approach that does not treat insurance policies as commodities but all as unique in their terms, conditions, and exclusions.

An approach that is not as much about spreadsheet price comparisons as it is about coverage nuances.

Not as much about budget as it is about the light at the end of the tunnel.

One that considers buying insurance as only one part of risk management.

A mentality of not shopping insurance among multiple brokers every year and instead choosing one that carefully evaluates insurance agencies, selects the most competent ones, and rides that horse with the insurance markets at the appropriate times.

Our vision is a kettle of fish that does not reward the "see you next year at renewal" concept of buying insurance but one where the broker is part of the team of managing risk with the other professionals of the company.

An approach that evaluates the agent not so much by the golf handicap but by the willingness to assume the responsibility of being more than an order-taker.

Differences that could result in your business continuing as a going concern or one that is referred to in the past tense.

An industry that offers a pledge like that of the Rigger's Pledge where those packing the insurance parachute are ready to jump with it.

Competence before crisis.

Resources Available to the Reader

Please look for other resources to assist you in the insurance-buying process at **www.packingyourparachute.com**

- Survey questions to evaluate insurance agents
- Sample assumption of special relationship agreement for use with agents
- Waivers of subrogation for lease agreements
- Insurance requirements in leases
- Insurance requirements in construction contracts
- Indemnification provision samples
- Template summaries of insurance
- List of verdicts and settlements since 2000
- Comparison between premises damage liability perils in CGL policies
- Checklist of common coverage gaps in business insurance programs
- Comparison of employment practices liability insurance policies
- Cyber insurance policy coverage checklist

NOTES

1. Daniel H. Pink, *To Sell is Human* (Riverhead Books, 2012).
2. https://www.inc.com/guides/2010/10/how-to-budget-for-business-insurance.html.
3. https://www.bls.gov/oes/current/oes413021.htm#(1).
4. MCL 500.2236(1).
5. http://www.iii.org/sites/default/files/docs/pdf/a_firm_foundation_2017.pdf.
6. http://www.naic.org/state_report_cards/report_card_wa.pdf.
7. O'Sullivan, Owen P., "The neural basis of always looking on the bright side." *Dialogues in Philosophy, Mental and Neuro Sciences*, 8, 1(2015): 11–15.
8. http://blog.willis.com/2012/04/insuring-the-titanic/; https://www.allianz.com/en/press/news/business/insurance/news_2012-03-27.html/.
9. http://www.titanicfacts.net/titanic-captain.html.
10. Mesa Underwriters Specialty Insurance Company, Plaintiff, v. Daniel Holman; Spica Holdings, LLC, a Delaware limited liability company; Frazier Land and Property, LLC, a California limited liability company; Scott F. Frazier. Defendants. United States District Court Eastern District of California.
11. Colony Insurance Company v. Troensa Construction Inc., Case 1:17-cv-03577-JBS-KMW (United States District Court for the District of New Jersey. 5/18/17).
12. http://www.jrlawfirm.com/blog/titanic-lawsuits/.
13. http://www.insurance.gov.ph/_@dmin/upload/reports/CL2016_30.pdf.
14. Florida statutes 626.9641.
15. Title 27, Chapter 12, Code of Alabama 1975; La.R.S. 22:41.
16. House Bill no. 1258, Mississippi.
17. MCL 500.2112.

INDEX

A

adjusters, 19–20, 23, 65
advisers, xv, xvii, 14–16, 32, 37, 42–43
A.M. Best, 7

B

bankruptcy, 56
bystander effect, iii, 31–33

C

claims, xii–xiii, xvii, 2–10, 13–14, 16–24, 26–29, 46, 48–49, 51, 53–54, 57, 61–62, 65, 69, 71, 73, 77–80, 84–85
  adjuster, 17, 19, 22
  crisis, xiv
  department, 19, 22
  history, 16, 48
  liability, 6, 77–78
  major, xii, 9, 21, 23
  payments, 7
  valid, 8
commissions, 41–42, 46, 48, 84
coverages, xiv, xvi–xvii, 5–6, 8, 10, 12–16, 19, 22, 24–25, 29, 32, 39–40, 42, 52, 54–56, 58, 63, 65, 67–70, 72, 79–81, 83–84
  business interruption, 20, 59, 63
  liability, 57, 69, 75

problems, xii, 39, 69
replacement cost, 25, 56, 62
customer service representatives (CSR), 49, 56

E

endorsements, xii, 2, 5–6, 12, 51, 68, 70, 80

F

Fitch, 7

G

Gross, Ethan, 19

I

insurance
  auto, 52
  automobile liability, 57
  building, 6
  business, iii, xi, xiii–xv, xviii, 9, 23, 33, 40, 45, 49, 51, 61, 72, 75, 82, 87, 89
  casualty, xiii, 42–43
  casualty business, 45
  certificate of, 56
  commercial, xiv, 4, 14, 37, 49
  cyber, 36
  environmental, 35

93

firm, 8
health, 46
liability, xvii, 6, 13, 57, 65–66, 70, 79
life, 23, 35
online, 53–55
property, 26, 52, 56, 59, 61, 65–68
insurance agencies, 7, 14, 40, 56, 82, 88
insurance audition, iii, xiii, 45–47
insurance carriers, 7–8, 42–43, 46–48, 53, 55, 72, 81
online, 53–54
insurance company, xvi–xvii, 6–7, 13, 15–17, 20–21, 24–26, 39, 53–54, 83–85
insurance department, 56, 83–84
insurance industry, xiii, xv–2, 16, 23, 65, 72
insurance markets, 81, 88
insurance programs, xi, xvii, 12, 65, 87
insurance protection, 72
insurance renewal, 75
Insurance Services Office (ISO), xvi, 6
insureds, xvi, xviii, 18–19, 28, 36, 61, 65–66, 69
Internal Revenue Service, 19

K

Kemper Insurance Company, 6–7

L

landlord, 18, 68, 70, 79
lease agreements, 32, 51, 77, 89
limited liability companies, 32, 67–68, 91
loss payees, 58, 65–68

M

misrepresentation, 8, 23–24

P

policies, xii–xviii, 2, 5, 9, 12–14, 16–25, 29–30, 33, 36, 40, 43, 46, 48, 51, 54, 56, 61–62, 65–68, 70–71, 79, 83–84, 87
disputes, 18
language, xii, xvi, 14, 18–20, 22, 25, 27, 80
umbrella, 33, 57, 70
policyholders, xv, xviii, 18–19, 24, 30, 53, 55, 57, 83–84
bill of rights of, iii, 83–84
premiums, xiii, xvii, 3, 7, 9, 19, 24, 26, 47, 66, 69, 71, 78
higher, xiii, 24
lowest, 46
property
commercial, 59
personal, 1, 56, 67, 76–77

R

rating, 7
risk management, xvii, 31, 33, 47–48, 72, 78, 81, 87
risks, xiii–xv, xvii–xviii, 4, 9, 19, 27, 31, 35, 45, 72–73, 75–81, 87
legal, xv

U

underwriters, xvi, 17, 22, 25, 53–54, 62, 72

www.ingramcontent.com/pod-product-compliance
Lightning Source LLC
Chambersburg PA
CBHW030848180526
45163CB00004B/1491